A Door Keeper in the House of the Lord

Dear Bill Carol,

You two have welcomed us back to Marietta. We are grateful for your love and friendship — and we loved St. Simons!

Rev. Joe Ev

Joe Evans

&

Parson's Porch Books

www.parsonsporchbooks.com

A Door Keeper in the House of the Lord
ISBN: Softcover 978-1- 949888-20-1
Copyright © 2018 by Joe Evans

I dedicate this book to Sara Evans.
"You're my blue sky, you're my sunny day."

Contents

Part 1 - Saying Goodbye and Hello with Romans

Part 2 - Philippians

Part 3 - Stewardship

Part 4 - From Christ the King of Christmas

Part 5 - The Season after Christmas

Part 6 - From Transfiguration Sunday to Easter

Part 7 - Ordinary Time

Introduction

On July 24, 2017, Rev. Joe Evans assumed the position of Senior Pastor at First Presbyterian Church of Marietta, Georgia. The timing of this was God's timing!

With the arrival of this man has come the sense of a great wind – a wind of excitement, enthusiasm, new energy, new dreams and planning, happiness, and love – sweeping over the congregation. This great Presbyterian church has endured extended times of difficult transition, with painful pruning; but finally now, there is unquestionable evidence of new growth. This church still holds on tight, though with a great big smile, as it experiences its very own Pentecostal gusts of Holy Spiritual reassurance! It has been phenomenal!

This preacher Joe Evans has a great and awesome talent – awesome in the sense that the Holy Spirit has Joe tightly in His grip – guiding him, yes, but letting him run ahead like a spirit-filled tiger on the loose.

First Presbyterian Church's Pastor Nominating Committee discovered quickly that this man, Joe Evans, has been respected and loved by all who have known him through schools, seminary, and each community in which he has served as pastor. This Marietta congregation has been ecstatic in witnessing its pastor's outright love for all, his humility, his great sense of fun, his energy, and his marvelous preaching. He is truly an anointed man. May God, and may we, help him to persevere in the living and preaching of His word. Joe is a part of the "Body of Christ" as is each of us. Let us do our part!

Allow me to make a couple of suggestions for reading this book. First, if the reader is not familiar with Rev. Joe Evans, please go online to fpcmarietta.org and into "Live Stream," and listen to or watch one or two recent sermons in order to have a better sense of his delivery. As you read, you then will enjoy a much better chance of "hearing" him preach. Secondly, keep a Bible close by to read the day's scriptures, which always precede his preaching.

May God speak to each one of us as we read His Scriptures and His words, spoken through this called preacher – a mortal like us who is trying to do his part in serving the Lord.

James Goodlet M.D.

With Gratitude

The sermons in this book were written with so much help from other people that I can hardly claim to be the author. Most every day I am taking notes as I see the Holy Spirit at work in the world, writing down things that I see and what I hear people say. I am very grateful for every person who has allowed me to share part of his or her story from the pulpit. Each of you has made the Gospel come alive to me.

It's also true that I never would have been a pastor at all were it not for the encouragement of many who saw something in me that I was unable to see myself. My parents, George and Cathy Evans, provided me every advantage, especially their unconditional love. My grandparents' pride was unrestrained and often undeserved.

I daily give thanks to God for my wife Sara, who from the very first time I met her, made me want to be a better man. And every night I pray that God might make me the kind of father that our two daughters need me to be. You all fill me with so much happiness that I am overcome by joy daily. Wherever we are, it feels like home when the four of us are together.

But there have been so many others to whom I give thanks: every English teacher who instilled in me a love for reading and writing, Mrs. Corley who taught me Sunday School in 3rd Grade, Jimmy Scarr who told me to keep a prayer in my back pocket because one never knew when he might be called on to pray, Dr. Peter Hobbie who was the first person to look me in the eye and tell me that I ought to consider being a pastor, Dr. Bob Stephens who kept up with me through seminary, and especially my first homiletics professor, Dr. Anna Carter Florence who heard my first sermon and told me I had a gift.

There have been Elders who embodied the magnitude of their title, and who held me up before I could stand on my own: Vivian Guthrie who installed me in three churches, David York who encouraged me to take a big step forward, Melinda Sanders who embodied grace, George Kesler who taught me how to moderate a session meeting and more, Don Crichton who lives the Gospel, Buck Buchanan who has guided me through the last year with love and patience, and so many others. I'll never forget the words of then Presbytery Executive, Bill Nesbit, who taught me to rely on the Session in times of crisis. No church would have survived me had I not been surrounded by men and women of faith and wisdom who modeled the Christian faith and made their churches strong.

Then there were pastors: Rev. Perky Daniels who baptized me, Dr. James O. Speed whom I revered, Rev. Robert Hay who trusted me as a leader of his youth group and showed me that ministers still get to have fun, Dr. Don Esa who led me through the ordination process, Rev. Stephanie Hankins with whom I first led worship, Rev. Dana Hughes who always cheers for me and looked me in the eye and told me that she thought God loved to hear me preach, Rev. Penny Hill who told me to let her be the president of my fan club because no one should be the president of his own fan club, Rev. Peter Wallace who asks the best questions, Dr. John Hinkle who walked beside me through a dark time, Dr. John Todd who sets the standard for what it means to be a cool pastor, Rev. Joe Brice who never fails to hold God's people in his heart, Dr. Todd Jones who is still a champion for our denomination, Dr. Henry Strock who is a giant in any pulpit, Dr. Erskine Clark who embodies the best of our tradition, Dr. Bill Williamson whose footsteps I was proud to follow, Dr. Maynard Pittendregh whom I was blessed to serve behind, Rev. Trent Ogilvie whom I will always be proud to have stood beside in the fight against racism, and I am doubly deeply grateful for the example of two pastors whom I am also blessed to be related to, Rev. Noble Miller and Dr. Lyn Pace. Thank you all for showing me what it means to be a pastor.

I have been blessed by every Sunday School teacher and Youth Group leader who nurtured me in the faith. I thank every church member who has listened to me as I've struggled to preach a good word and who encouraged me to keep going. I am blessed to be held up in prayer by many, but constantly am I encouraged by Tim Jones, who for over a year, each Sunday morning at 6:00 AM has sent me a Scripture verse. I give thanks to God for all of you.

I have been honored to do ministry beside many gifted church staff members. So many of you are like family, and I have been blessed by your love. In you I have also been reminded that ours is not a job but a calling.

Thanks are due to editors and proofreaders Martha and Jim Goodlet. You two are like family to us, and we are all thankful for you. I thank David Russell Tullock and all the staff at *Parson's Porch Book Company*. Without you this book would not exist. And were it not for Wanda Reese who asked for this book before it was a possibility, I might never have taken the invitation to publish a collection of my sermons seriously.

Finally, I'm exceedingly grateful and honored by the pastor nominating committees who interviewed me and discerned that I was called by God to serve in their churches. Jim Hodges, James Fleming, Dr. Jim Goodlet, and their committees will never know what a privilege it has been to have gained their trust. And you three men, each in your own way, affirmed my call to preach. This is a call that I've frequently doubted. I know that if it were not for the three of you I would not be where I am today. Your love and your encouragement are gifts that I give thanks to God for daily.

Preface

The sermons included in this book were written and preached by me after I was called to be Senior Pastor at First Presbyterian Church, Marietta, Georgia. The first two sermons represent my farewell to the First Presbyterian Church congregation in Columbia, Tennessee and subsequent sermons were prepared and preached in Marietta, from the time of my arrival in July of 2017 through the date of my first year anniversary.

As a child of First Presbyterian Church of Marietta, a call to return as Pastor was a gift that brought back many memories for me. The preacher I grew up listening to, Dr. James O. Speed, still sings in the choir every Sunday, and as the two of us have now switched chairs, I've been reminded of something he told me when I graduated seminary: "Being a pastor's not so hard, Joe. All I've had to do is keep the doors open and avoid doing anything too stupid."

Those words of his, and certainly his example that I witnessed as a child in the congregation he faithfully served, inspire my ministry today and inspired the title of this book: *A Door Keeper in the House of the Lord.*

What does the stole that the preacher wears symbolize but that we are the chief foot-washer of the church we serve, and what does it mean to me to be a pastor now as I serve the Lord in the church in which I grew up? While I am called to sit in the big fancy chair at the front of the Sanctuary, my call is simply to keep the doors open and to point to the one whose love changes everything!

It is a gift to proclaim the Gospel. Every time I stand behind the pulpit, I am overcome by the privilege of it.

Part 1

Saying Goodbye and Hello with Romans

The following two sermons are the last two I preached while serving First Presbyterian Church of Columbia, Tennessee. After six and a half years of living there with my wife and two daughters and being embraced by this loving community, Columbia felt like home. As our girls were so young when we moved there, Columbia was the only place they had known, and First Presbyterian was the only church they had known. But in the spring of 2017, the church in which I grew up, First Presbyterian Church of Marietta, Georgia, called me to be their new pastor, and the push of the Holy Spirit was too strong to deny.

During the following series of sermons on passages from Romans, I say goodbye to one church and hello to another.

Justified
Exodus 19:2-8a and Romans 5:1-8

The title of this morning's sermon is Justified - a one-word title that I chose deliberately because this is the subject of my sermon today – justification or to be justified.

This is my next to last sermon here, and I'm taking this Sunday's sermon and next Sunday's sermon to preach about two essential Christian principles – justification and sanctification – so the sermon title today is "Justified". The sermon title for next Sunday is "Sanctified".

Clear enough, right?

Well, it's clear enough if you know what being justified means. People use this word. Christians use this word. Maybe you've heard it in church or in a court of law, but of course, you know that people use words without knowing what they mean all the time – take for example the word superfluous. I used that word in a sermon two weeks ago, but Sara told me that I used it incorrectly, so I used it again last Sunday just to redeem myself.

Predestination is a word that Presbyterians are supposed to know a little something about, but I'd rather not be put on the spot to talk about it, and justification is another theological term – this one of crucial importance – but you just about must read a book on the subject to understand what it means.

Justified. What do I mean when I say justified?

Or, more importantly, what did Paul mean when he wrote the word justified?

Our Second Scripture Lesson began: "Therefore, since we are justified by faith, we have peace with God through our Lord Jesus Christ, through whom we have obtained access to this grace in which we stand; and we boast in our hope of sharing the glory of God."

You can tell from just this passage that being justified is about Grace, and Grace is a word that we all know well.

Amazing grace, how sweet the sound,
that saved a wretch like me!
I once was lost, but now am found,
was blind but now I see.

Being justified is about standing before God, not as one condemned, but as one forgiven. Justification is about salvation, how it works, what it means, what it is that Jesus has done for you and me.

Justification is the difference between this religion that we call Christianity and a religion that masquerades as Christianity in popular culture that I'll call moralism. Moralism is all about being good, doing right, following the rules, and doing so enough of the time that you get to go to Heaven.

That sounds a lot like Christianity. In fact, I'd wager that if you asked most Christians to describe their religion, that's about what they'd tell you. They might say, "I go to church to learn how to live, so that on judgment day I'm deemed worthy of entrance through those Pearly Gates."

But Christianity is not about worthiness.

Moralism is all about being good enough, and Christianity is about knowing that you're not, you never were, and you never will be good enough, but God loves you still.

If moralism is about goodness, then Christianity is about grace.

And if moralism is about being good enough to go to heaven, then Christianity is about knowing that heaven is ours not because we are good, but because we're justified.

Moralism is the religion of the school classroom, the courthouse, and the dentist – it's all about whether you have listened well enough, followed the rules enough, and flossed your teeth enough. Moralism is about measuring up to certain standards – and I don't mean that moralism is foreign to Christianity, but Christianity is more than that. Christianity goes beyond measuring up to provide you with this Good News: that if you know that you never have and that you never will attain perfection, rest in the assurance that what you can't do for yourself God has done for you.

Speaking of measuring up, or trying to measure up, yesterday I had to drive down to Dalton, Georgia.

You might know this – that for a Presbyterian minister to serve a church in a different region, a different presbytery, he or she must be examined by the pastors and elders of that presbytery and receive their approval – to see if he or she measures up.

I've been through the process three times now: once to begin ministry at Good Shepherd Presbyterian Church outside Atlanta, a second time to begin ministry here in Columbia, and now a third time I've been examined so that I can begin ministry at First Presbyterian Church of Marietta, Georgia.

So, I've just been examined by a presbytery who knew me when I was a child … and as a teenager.

There, with the right to ask whatever question they wanted, were people who remember me when I was 7 or 8, disrupting Sunday School class. There were people there who knew me when I was 16 years old, driving around Marietta, Georgia in a car painted in black and white checkerboard. They wanted to know if I was up to the challenge of a new church. This is a hard question to answer, because I've never felt worthy of serving the church I serve now.

Yesterday there was no pretending: I have not always been a pristine example of being good, nor am I now, nor will I ever be.

Yesterday, I didn't need to pretend that I could measure up to the standards that some put on the office of pastor, because they knew already that I couldn't. Instead, I stood as another example of one who has been justified by the mighty work of God in Christ Jesus, for I am a sinner who has received God's grace.

The Pope said it best. When Pope Francis was asked to describe himself, he said, "I am a sinner." And knowing that we cannot do any better, what good is it to pretend to be innocent when we know we have failed to measure up?

However, while we may have failed to measure up, we do not stand condemned.

We stand justified. Justified by faith, because our Lord Jesus Christ, by his death on a cross, gives us peace with God. Through him we obtain access to grace, so if we boast, we cannot boast in ourselves. For what have we done? We can only boast in what Christ has done on our behalf.

To use the words of Rev. Diane Givens Moffett, Senior Pastor at St. James Presbyterian Church in Greensboro, North Carolina: "We cannot win God's favor. We need only accept God's grace."

And maybe that sounds easy, but it's hard. It's especially hard if you're not used to it.

Father's Day is today, and maybe you have a father who helped you remember just how far you had to go before you measured up. Maybe you had a father you're still trying to measure up to.

You got a part in the play, but he wanted you to play football.

The closest he came to saying he loved you was a handshake and a pat on the back.

When you graduated High School, maybe you had a father who, instead of telling you how proud he was, asked you why you didn't graduate with honors.

Some of us think of God this way. If God is our Father in Heaven, then some imagine that surely He remembers that summer when we wrecked his car and is still holding it against us. Preachers preach this way, and I once believed them, but there are many ways to be a father, and it's important to know the kind of Father that our God is.

A preacher named Ray Jones told it this way: he was walking his daughter down the aisle at her wedding. She told him again and again, "Daddy, just don't make me cry. Don't say anything that will make me cry at my wedding."

So, he kept his mouth shut through the rehearsal dinner. Didn't give a toast or anything, but as he walked her down the aisle, he whispered to her, "I love you, and if you live to be a thousand years old, you will still never fully know the gift you are to your mother and me."

If God is our Father in Heaven, is God not this kind of father?

The kind whose love for us, in just a few simple words, brings tears to our eyes?

What does it mean to be justified – it means that whatever you've done, wherever you've been, no matter how far you've gone – your Heavenly Father is waiting with open arms to welcome you home.

To be justified is to remember that the God of the Exodus is still delivering His people from slavery out of profound and powerful love.

To be justified is to know that the price of your imperfection has already been paid by a loving Savior who laid down his life that you might know what a father's love truly is meant to be.

Now that doesn't mean we can do whatever we want. That doesn't mean we should wallow around in sin and debauchery – but that's next Sunday's sermon – sanctification.

For now, for today, remember this – you might not have been enough, you might never be enough, but God is, and God always will be, with grace enough to cover all our sin.

That's justification.

Thanks be to God. Amen.

Sanctified
Jeremiah 20:7-13 and Romans 6:1-11

My grandmother, my mother's mother, was a wonderful person.

She died in the first year that I was here, and while we had only been here a few months there were those of you who gave memorial gifts in her honor. I can't really say how much that gesture meant to me.

I remember her fondly, and she was a character.

She worked as a labor and delivery nurse for 50 years, and so dedicated herself to her work that she developed no hobbies other than shopping. Her favorite store was a place called Shamricks. It's a place full of knick-knacks and potpourri. It's one of the levels of Hell in Dante's Inferno to a 12-year-old boy, and I was there often with her at that age, walking through aisles, trying to understand how my grandmother could spend so much time in a place like that.

From Shamricks my grandmother purchased a cat. It wasn't alive or anything – it was decorative. A little cat curled in on itself for people like my grandmother to decorate their beds with. Before Sara and I were married, when we'd visit my grandmother, Sara was always asked to sleep in the master bedroom in the big, king-sized bed. This bed was decorated with hundreds of pillows and this one cat curled up like it was sleeping, that Sara would kick onto the floor and bury under the pillows because she was sure the thing was going to come alive at any minute.

Sara is smart. Perceptive. And it isn't surprising that she was pretty much right about the cat. It was front-page news in the local paper: "Shamricks sells stuffed Chinese alley cats to area residents." As soon as my grandmother heard about it, that these decorative cats of hers, had in fact, at one time, been real cats, she rushed over to her favorite store and spoke to the cashier.

"Good morning," she said.

And that's all it took for the cashier to start apologizing: "Mrs. Bivens, we're so sorry about those cats. We're just mortified. I hope you can see past this horrible mistake. We've already packed the ones we had left and we're ready to ship them back where they came from."

"So, you haven't sent them back yet," my grandmother said. "In that case, could you go back there and get me a couple more? I need them for the guest bedrooms."

That's about my favorite story.

And it's funny, because if you know better, if you know the decorative cats are real cats, you shouldn't buy any more.

If you know better, you shouldn't.

It's like chitlins – if you know what they are, you shouldn't eat them, but I do.

And it's like sin – if you've been saved from it, forgiven of it, then you shouldn't sin anymore, but considering what we've learned about justification, what's to keep us from doing it?

Many churches don't preach the kind of justification that you heard preached last Sunday. In some churches, a warning is preached: don't you sin, or Hell awaits.

In those churches you avoid sin and you do what is right so you can avoid eternal punishment, but we're not that kind of a church. We believe what Paul wrote in Romans chapter 5: that Christ has saved us – that we're justified – and it's not our work that's going to get us into heaven; it's what Christ has done for us.

But, without the fear of eternal punishment, what's to keep us from returning to a life of sin?

That's the question Paul is trying to answer in Romans chapter 6 – if salvation is all about grace, then why live a righteous life? Why be sanctified?

Or, in other words, when you take out the fear part – it's hard to get some people to do the right thing. Think about home inspections.

We've been getting our house in order these past couple weeks. After having a bathroom renovated, we had to have a final inspection, and one inspector came over and he gave me a punch list of five or six things he wanted done.

I wanted to pass the inspection, so it didn't matter what he asked for – out of a fear of failing I installed something called a Studor valve and a bunch of other stuff. A couple of neighbors helped. I watched some do-it yourself videos, made 5 or 6 visits to Lowe's, spent a handful of money and wore myself out for a day and a half to get all this stuff done. Well, the inspector came back after I finished, but it was a different inspector this time. This new inspector walked into the bathroom, turned on the water in the sink, made sure the toilet flushed and we passed.

She didn't even look at my Studor valve.

Now what is the point of doing right and living right if we've already passed the test?

That's what Paul's critics wanted to know, so here's what Paul told them and what he now tells us: while our eternity is secured by our Lord Jesus Christ – what hangs in the balance is how we will live today, so he asked: "How can we who died to sin go on living in it?"

One of our finest teachers took me out to Puckett's last week. Mr. Mark Bridges is his name and he told me that parents call him often about grades. They want to know why their son is failing or why their daughter, who has a 99% doesn't have 100%. "This is frustrating," he said, "because people call about grades and why don't they call worried about whether their children are learning?"

Will we learn anything without grades?

Will we keep our bathrooms up to code without inspectors?

Will we live righteous lives without fear of eternal punishment?

That's the question that Paul answers here in Romans chapter 6, and that's what sanctification is all about – "How can we who died to sin go on living in it?"

If all we want to do is pass the class then we can sleep while the teacher is talking, but is school not more than grades? Is righteousness not more than just doing what you should? Is the burden of sin not a punishment in and of itself?

So much of life is about trying to prove ourselves – and justification takes the struggle away. By what we've done and left undone, we've proven that we deserve condemnation, but in Christ's saving death we've been redeemed and forgiven. Now the struggle is over – by grace you and I have been saved and there's only one reason to do what is right. Not because we should, not because there's some great big judgmental Father in Heaven looking down and wagging His finger. No. Do what is right because it's worth it.

Floss – not because you should, not because the dentist will get angry, but because teeth come in handy.

Be honest – not because you'll go to Hell if you lie, but because those who live a lie are strangers even to themselves.

Live in love – not because your mother raised you to be a good little boy or girl, but because hate is too great a burden to bear.

This is sanctification – this act of living a righteous life, not because we can earn our way into heaven. Christ has already justified us. Heaven is ours because of Him – but live a righteous life because there is no better way to live and because there is no better way to thank our God for the gift of creating us and redeeming us than living by God's great laws of love.

You might remember that legendary question and answer from the Westminster Shorter Catechism:

Q. What is the chief end of man?

A. Man's chief end is to glorify God, and to enjoy him forever.

To enjoy Him. To enjoy the fruits of a sanctified life.

To benefit from a healthy marriage. To rejoice in loving friendships.

To live filled up by an abiding peace that guilt nor hardship can touch.

We forget that God tells us to love one another, not because we should, but because there is no more miserable person than the one who only thinks of himself.

You see – sin is its own enslavement. Sin is death enough on its own. Remember that.

I just want to leave here knowing that you know two things:

1. That you are justified, not by anything that you've done, but by what God has done.
2. That you must grow in righteousness, you must live the sanctified life, because there is no other way to live.

What Christ has done is given this gift of eternal life – you are justified; and by living according to His commands, we can have the benefit of that eternal life today. Be sanctified.

Love the Lord your God with all your heart, soul, and mind, and love your neighbor as yourself. In six and a half years, I've never said anything more important than that.

And we do so, not out of a place of fear, wondering where we'll go when we die. We do it because what else could we do?

When you think of what God has done for us – how could we live any other way.

And that's what motivates us to do all great things – it's love, not fear.

I want to be a good father to my children, not out of obligation, but because I love them so much.

I want to be a loving husband to Sara, not out of obligation, or even because she's stronger than I am and could probably take me in a fight, but because when I think of her my heart fills up.

And I have worked to be a good pastor, not just because you've paid me to, not just because I should, but because I love you, and I want everyone whom I love to have a pastor who works to preach the truth and to stand by the bedside.

It's never been an obligation to baptize your children or to preach at your weddings.

It's never been a burden to speak at a funeral – it's only ever been an honor.

This is sanctification – living a righteous, loving life, not just because we should, or someone told us to, but because love drives us to it.

Amen.

Great and Steadfast Love
1 Kings 3:5-12 and Romans 8:26-39

As you know, school starts on Thursday, and starting a new school year is no small thing.

It's no small thing for a teacher, it's no small thing for a parent, it's no small thing for a student, especially those students who are starting the year, not only in a new class, but also in a new school.

Certain things are of crucial importance this week for these students.

Namely, what will you wear? And second to that, do you have the necessary school supplies?

School supplies are serious business.

You make a statement with your school supplies.

When grown-ups meet other grown-ups, they're sizing each other up according to clothes and cars and diamond earrings, but when you're in 3rd grade it comes down to the contents of pencil cases and lunch boxes.

Back in Middle School there was this one kid whose mom wouldn't buy him name brand Oreos and he got called "Generic Eric" from 6th grade on.

Can you believe that?

It's true. I'm sorry to say I was one of them.

Kids can be mean. People can be mean, so it's important to show up with the right stuff. Our church is a part of making sure that this happens. I'm proud of any number of things that I've learned about our church's ministry to this community. Every day I've come into the church this week this Great Hall has been filled with sack lunches for children in our community. Before that, I know there was a drive that you participated in to collect school supplies.

This is good work, because it's hard to start school. It's hard to enter a new classroom with a new teacher, but it's worse if you already know you don't have the right stuff. It's worse if you already feel behind because you don't have the bottle of glue and box of colored pencils or whatever it is that everyone else seems to have.

School starts this week and new students — I know that you want to be ready. I want you to be ready. Your parents want you to be ready, so today, if they haven't before now, parents will be taking you to Staples or some place to buy you everything on that list. No one wants to feel unprepared on their first day of school.

Everyone wants to look like they have it all together. That everything is just right. That they're ready. And that's true for the first day of school and that's true of every day after that — we are all trying to look like we have it all together.

But education takes more than that.

Wisdom takes more than being prepared and having it all together. Look at Solomon.

Can you imagine what it must have been like to be Solomon?

It was when I was in third grade that we moved here to Marietta from Atlanta. I was a new student at Hickory Hills Elementary School, and as you know, Marietta is one of those great places where some families have deep roots. It's like this church where a person could be a member for 20 years and still feel like they just got here. Hickory Hills was that way. Some of the teachers had been there for a while, so I was jealous as Ms. Cook, my 5th grade teacher, called role and told Andrew Breshears that she had taught his brother and sister. Told Molly Dykes that her big sister had been such an excellent student and that she knew she could expect the same from her.

This is one of those wonderful things about a community with real ties. You can feel at home among new acquaintances because they know your people, and that's good. I like that. As a child I remember wanting that, but deep roots can be a problem too, because sometimes people who know you well can know you too well.

Dr. Jim Goodlet chaired the Pastor Nominating Committee that interviewed me. He and the entire committee have been incredible. I could not be more grateful for them and their hard work, but soon after you voted to call me here as your new Senior Pastor Jim told me that the Joe Evans stories are really flowing. "Everyone is talking about what they remember of you from when you were in High School" he said, and it was in that moment that I really got nervous.

It can be a wonderful thing to be known.

It can be a wonderful thing for people to know you before they meet you.

It can be a wonderful thing to be remembered. For people to think well of you because of your older siblings, your grandparents, your mother or your father, so long as your father kept his dark secrets to himself.

What would it have been like to be Solomon?

If Solomon were a new student on his first day of school and if we think of God as a mighty cosmic school teacher then surely as Solomon stood there before the all-knowing Creator of Heaven and Earth who knew his father David and knew what David had done, then could Solomon possibly have felt as though he had it all together?

To stand before God as he did in our First Scripture Lesson from the book of 1 Kings – what would it have been like, not only to stand before the one who created you, who was there forming you in your mother's womb, who knows your going in and your coming out, your inward parts and the number of hairs on your head – but not only that – who knows what your daddy did when he looked down from his roof and saw from the roof a woman bathing.

You know the story too.

King David, Solomon's father, saw Bathsheba, called for her.

Her husband was away at war.

So, Solomon stands before God in our First Scripture Lesson, and if this were his first day of School, if God were his new teacher, what would God say?

"Good morning Solomon. I know your father. I remember what he did, so please excuse yourself from my presence."

Some wouldn't be surprised if that were the case. That's what happens all the time, so that's what some of us expect to happen.

If you slip, if you fall, if your father fell – your name may well be left off the list, wiped from the roll.

I wonder if that's what happened to Bill.

Last I lived here in Marietta, Georgia I used to go eat at a place called Bill and Louise's. Bill's name has been stricken from the record – painted right over. Apparently, he died, but I don't see how Louise can be so upset at him for that.

It's not always known what we've done or not done, said or didn't say, but be sure of this, some people will turn their back on you because they know you don't have it all together.

You know that's true and so do I, but the question is, while some people will paint right over your name, is that what you'll do? Is that what God does?

Consider Romans chapter 8. Has anything better ever been written?

For years I thought of God as some great heavenly fifth grade teacher who had me marked for a troublemaker and a miscreant.

For years I thought of God as some great heavenly Louise who would any minute paint over my name should I slip and fall.

But listen to this. Just listen to it: "For I am convinced that neither death, nor life, nor angels, nor rulers, nor things present, nor things to come, nor powers, nor height, nor depth, nor anything else in all creation, will be able to separate us from the love of God in Christ Jesus our Lord."

Did you get that?

Maybe not, because you've heard the opposite so many times before.

I heard the opposite so I'm sure you heard it.

You've heard the idolatry – of the God who removes favor, who picks favorites, who is with you one day walking beside you but who drops you down into the fires of Hell the next. You've heard of that human invention conceived by parents to scare children and advertised by preachers to inspire repentance, but how could such an image be true when it runs so contrary to what the Bible says here in the 8th chapter of the book of Romans?

We stand before God just as Solomon did. We stand before the Lord as broken, imperfect people who have failed to live up to our own expectations, but does that render us as sheep to be slaughtered?

No.

"In all things, we are more than conquerors" because the one who loves us is greater than all the powers of Hell, all the powers of earth, all our deepest regrets, and even our darkest shame.

That's what I can see today, because once again you are teaching it to me.

It started in third grade – the Corley's were my Sunday School teachers.

And from then on, we sang songs. We used to sing this one that went: "I am a promise, I am a possibility, I am a promise, with a capitol P. I am a great big bundle of potentiality."

And that was true, but we changed the p's to t's and sang it that way. Why? Because we take potential and we squander it on mischief.

Take the pink chairs that used to be in here – you remember them?

One summer Paul Sherwood, the man who used to be in Andy Workman's office – he hired David Elliot and me to shampoo the pink chairs. I remember the maintenance man saying that some of them were so dirty it's like a 5-year-old had been sitting in them with a pork chop in one hand and an ice cream cone in the other.

Well, for five dollars an hour we took stacks of those pink chairs outside by the railroad tracks, and we'd shampoo for a while, but then we'd get bored, so we'd look for things to put on the railroad tracks. The best was a can of spray paint. Have you ever seen a train run over a can of spray paint? It's incredible – but don't ever do it.

What I'm trying to say here is this: I stand before you as Solomon stood before God – I can't pretend. I can't hide what I'm ashamed of. You know me, and you know that it's just me up here, but still you've called me to be your pastor. Still you're here listening to what I have to say, and once again you're teaching me what you've taught me before – that love isn't something you can turn on and off. If you love people you have to take them as they are – warts and all – so knowing that you love me, let me be honest enough to say that it's the first day of school for me and I don't have all my school supplies ready.

In fact, I can just barely get in and out of my office and I have yet to successfully print anything from my computer on my own.

That's why I take considerable comfort from Solomon today, because here he shows me that wisdom is one of those wonderful things that you only receive when you admit that you don't have it already.

He said: "And now, O Lord my God, you have made your servant king in place of my father David, although I am only a little child; I do not know how to go out or come in. [So] give your servant therefore an understanding mind."

We are all trying to look like we have it all together. This week at school, as much as we can, we want our children to walk into their new classrooms with all the supplies that they need already placed in their cute little backpacks – we want them to be ready – but let us also encourage them to admit that they are not ready, that they don't know, and they don't have to have it all together because no one does.

There are so many things in this life that we only receive when we stop pretending that we have them: wisdom, for one … and forgiveness for another.

Have you ever heard an apology from someone who wasn't quite ready to admit that they needed forgiveness?

It's like a student who isn't quite ready to admit that he doesn't already know.

But if we are here it is because we know that we are in need – in need of a savior who can bring us the salvation that we could never earn for ourselves. Who can take us, our brokenness and can put us together.

Thanks be to God that He is ours and we are His.

Amen.

Come to the Waters
Isaiah 55:1-5 and Romans 9:1-5

It is such an incredible gift to be here. I have loved relearning this church, amazed all over again at the scope of our ministry. I walked into the Great Hall two weeks ago. The whole backside of that huge room was covered in sack lunches.

The members of our church who volunteered must have assembled thousands of lunches for kids in our community. It was incredible.

Certainly, I can see that a lot has changed around here. But some things have stayed the same, and our determination to serve this community seems to have stayed the same.

Another thing that's the same: on Thursday, I received a note from Andrea Freund that said, "Drive by High School to see toilet paper memories." It took me a second to realize what she meant, but if you drove by the High School on Thursday or Friday or if you saw the front page of Marietta Daily Journal Friday morning then you know what she was talking about. Again, I can see that a lot has changed around here, but some things have stayed the same.

Marietta High School Seniors are still wasting hundreds and thousands of rolls of toilet paper by throwing it into trees and through arches to cover their High School in soft, white, toilet tissue. But some things change, and what has changed is the administration's reaction. Did you see that Principle Gabe Carmona, according to the Marietta Daily Journal, called the event "A great bonding experience for the class of 2018"? And then new superintendent of schools, Grant Rivera, cooked out Wednesday night at the High School ahead of the rolling party, and said, "It's an almost 60-year tradition, something school administrators want to embrace."

This is new.

According to the paper, when Mary Ansley Southerland, daughter of the late Mayor Ansley Meaders, was a senior out late at night with toilet paper filling her mother's Cadillac, she was pulled over by the police. That experience is much more like my own. At that time, I drove a checkerboard Chevrolet and believe it or not, after seeing the school the night we filled the trees with toilet paper, the police thought my friends and I had something to do with it. The next day the principal had us pick up toilet paper all morning. He made an example of us...not a good example either, so this business of seniors being allowed to roll Marietta High School is new. Some things change, others stay the same. The tradition of High School Seniors decorating the High School with toilet paper is still alive and well, but what has changed is how the administration deals with it, and that change is significant because how we deal with people, how we speak to them, especially when they're not doing what we think they should, matters tremendously.

Consider people who don't attend Church, ours or anyone else's.

In the time between serving First Presbyterian Church in Columbia, Tennessee and coming here I had several Sundays off. On one occasion, I was at Home Depot at 11:00 Sunday morning. Now that hasn't always been possible, but there I was, and a whole bunch of other people were there too. None of us were in a church; we were all at Home Depot, which is a strange phenomenon.

They say that there was a time when everything was closed on Sunday, because everyone was in a church – that's changed – and all at once we have these people, young and old, black and white, rich and poor, who don't necessarily think of going to a church on Sunday morning, and might not be able to tell you why they should.

The question for Presbyterians is this: what should we do?

How can we get more folks out of Home Depot and into a sanctuary?

Some would say that this is an issue that Presbyterians have always had a hard time with. There's a great joke – what do you get when you mix a Jehovah's Witness with a Presbyterian?

Someone who knocks on your door but doesn't know what to say.

What should we say? According to Peter, "We must all be ready to give an account of the hope that is in us." And, likewise, Paul writes here in Romans chapter 9, not a biting opinion piece raking atheists and backsliders across the coals, but here he offers words of lamentation to his brothers and sisters who do not believe, saying in this morning's Second Scripture Lesson something very close to: "Don't you know what you're missing out on?"

Isn't that something? And isn't that something different from the ways that many of our brothers and sisters in Christ are relating to those who haven't been to a church in a while? In the middle of July on the marquee out front a church right here in Cobb County were the words: "You think it's hot now?"

The Church as fire insurance is what that is – the Church as deliverance from Hell. Some churches offer that and consider any who would darken the doors of a Home Depot as on the road, not to home improvement, but to fire and brimstone. Others take a page out of the medical profession's play book, so after worship on Sunday you feel about the same way you do when you leave the dentist's office: "You know, I really should do better. I really should be better." I should, I should, I should and there's truth in that – we all should be better, we all should do better. Who in this sacred room doesn't have an area of his life that he'd like to improve, but is that what the Church is? Is that the message we want to send?

Sometimes the Church sounds like the angry citizens of our community reacting to a High School covered in toilet paper: "It's just a shame what they've done," and maybe it is, but shame – sometimes shame does far more harm than good. Paul wrote to his brothers and sisters, the Jews, and this is what he said: "I have great sorrow and unceasing anguish in my heart. For I could wish that I myself were accursed and cut off from Christ for the sake of my own people, my kindred according to the flesh." Isn't that beautiful?

Paul knows the abundant life that they, his own people, are missing out on. And he so desires that they know the joy that he has in his heart, that in Christ like love he wishes to sacrifice himself for their sake. This is love – not guilt or obligation. Before that we heard from the Prophet Isaiah: "Everyone who thirsts, come to the waters. Why do you spend your money for that which is not bread, and your labor for that which does not satisfy? Listen carefully to me, and eat what is good, and delight yourselves in rich food" because here we have all that the world is searching for, working for, spending their way into debt in the hopes of finding. Here we have the water for the thirsty and the food for eternal life, but all so many churches are advertising to the world is either Hell or guilt.

A lot has changed, but some things have stayed the same, and I say that because even though there's Snapchat and Facebook and Instagram, these new technologies are promising the same thing that people have been thirsting for since the beginning: acceptance, love, friendship, and community. A woman named Diane Maloney brought that to light for me. She still serves the church I did in Columbia, Tennessee, and she told me that what technology promises – namely connection – technology cannot provide.

You've witnessed it – you know someone who has 500 friends on Facebook, but not a single person to call when he needs help moving.

There's another who works so hard to put together the perfect pictures for Instagram but has no one to talk to about the feeling of inadequacy she just can't shake.

35

Technology promises connection – but haven't you seen the couple who sits there looking at their phones, ignoring the human being who sits on the other side of table? This abundant life of connection – to quench our thirst for community and our longing for satisfaction – Apple is trying to sell what the Church has been giving away for 2,000 years.

A lot has changed, but some things have stayed the same – this table is the same. The Gospel is the same. The love of God is the same – and we, as Christians, must preach love, hope, community, and forgiveness, leaving fear and judgment behind. So, if you find the love and acceptance that feeds your heart here, I pray you won't keep such a gift as this to yourself. The deep longing of our human heart has always been the same – it's as true for me as it is for everyone who is at Home Depot this very minute. What has changed is that so many have forgotten that they'll only find what they're looking for in a place like this one. That's why we must tell them, "Come to the waters, and find rest for your soul."

Amen.

How Beautiful are the Feet?
1 Kings 19:9-18 and Romans 10:5-15

This has been a big week for me at the Church office – I emptied my last box. I am fully moved in – you are stuck with me. As I unpacked my last box, I remembered what my friend James Fleming said back in Columbia, Tennessee. He was there as I was packing my books into the boxes I had picked up at the liquor store and he said, "I'm not here to say goodbye because it won't be long before they send you back up here, showing up looking like you have a serious drinking problem."

James is a wise man, and he was worried about how I might be perceived. Perception is something that we all are worried about or ought to be worried about. That's because as we go through life people take a good look at us. They see how we choose to present ourselves, the boxes we chose to pack up our books in, and begin making assumptions.

I'm not sure how one would define the word assumption, but I do know that assumptions are important. While they're not always accurate, they're accurate enough of the time that they should be taken seriously. For example – if a restaurant has been given a failing score by the Health Department you don't need to investigate further to determine the quality of the food, but, if a person has tattoos on her arms or a cigarette hanging from her lips, one might make a completely inaccurate assumption about the quality of her heart.

Let me give you an example – I was once driving through Chattanooga on the way to Columbia, Tennessee from a funeral in Stone Mountain. I waited too long to stop for gas, so I had to pull off the interstate on an undesirable exit. It was dark, the gas station was not well lit, I noticed a creaky old Buick parked by the convenience store, motor still running. Wondering why someone would leave the motor running in this part of town, I jumped out of the car quickly, hustled to the pump only to realize that I had left my wallet in the car. I had changed out of my suit and into shorts before starting back home, and as I was leaning over the driver's seat to reach my wallet, I heard the Buick shift into gear and then a raspy woman's voice began shouting: "Young man! Young man!"

I hoped she wasn't talking to me, but she was. I was thankful I didn't have any cash because by the sound of her voice I knew that I would have given her all of it if she would just leave me alone.

I cautiously turned around and the lady says, "Young man! You sure have nice legs."

With that she drove off.

Assumptions.

Based on my assumptions alone I had prepared myself for a conversation much less pleasant than that one, and that's how assumptions are – they're important because sometimes they're right. But other times they'll keep you from interactions that bring joy to creepy old gas stations and can sometimes stop meaningful relationships before they even begin.

We must be careful about assumptions.

Sometimes, what's required is more research, more data, more investigation. Consider Elijah. Just before the events described in our First Scripture Lesson take place, he asked that he might die saying, "It is enough; now, O Lord, take away my life, for I am no better than my ancestors." That's a state of hopelessness based on an assumption. Based on his observations he was a failure abandoned by God. He battled King Ahab and Queen Jezebel, fighting for reform in a time of belligerent governance. He remained faithful in a time when idolatry was convenient. He spoke out in truth in a time when no one wanted to hear the truth, which is the kind of thing that will wear you out after a while. So, having hit a wall, having sunk down into a state of fear for his own life, he surrendered, abandoned his mission, vacated his position. Elijah ran away.

You know what this is like. It's in times of unemployment, infertility, cancer treatment – those dark nights where we knock and knock and knock on a door that no one ever answers. It's in those time when we pour our days and our nights into the pursuit of something important only to be left empty that we assume that the world would be better off had we never tried. But into his dark night a voice spoke: "Go out and stand on the mountain before the Lord; for the Lord is about to pass by."

Then there was a great wind, so strong that it was splitting mountains and breaking rocks in pieces, but the Lord was not in the wind. Then there was an earthquake, but the Lord was not in the earthquake. And after the earthquake a fire, but the Lord was not in the fire.

What you need to know about the wind, the earthquake, and the fire is that the Lord had revealed himself in these three ways to the Israelites more than once. From Moses, who saw God in the burning bush and the great pillar of fire, Elijah knew to look for God in the fire. Likewise, Scripture tells us that in the time of the Judges, God spoke through earthquakes and wind, so Elijah knew to look and listen for God in earthquakes and wind. But this time – this time the Lord was in neither the fire, the earthquake, nor the wind. This time God came to Elijah in the sound of sheer silence, which is not the place anyone would have assumed that God would be.

When Elijah heard it, he wrapped his face in his mantle and went out and stood at the entrance of the cave. Then there came a voice to him that said, "What are you doing here Elijah? Not preaching the truth in Israel, but hiding out in a cave, what are you doing here? Not standing for what is right at the palace, but huddled in the dark, what are you doing here? Not expecting to find me at work in the world, but assuming I had abandoned you and your people, what are you doing here?"

I know where here is. Don't you?

I wasn't in a cave. For me it was on a subway train in New York City. For a week one summer during college I was able to attend a type of mission trip up there. We spent our time feeding the homeless in all different types of shelters and soup kitchens. This was the first time my eyes had really been opened to just how many people are living their life without even a roof over the heads, and what hurt my heart the most was how little anyone could do about it.

All these shelters.

All these soup kitchens.

All these agencies, but once you're living on the street without a phone or an address, you almost can't get a job because you can't be contacted for an interview.

It's just so overwhelming how hard it is to get back on your feet once you're down. All these people, living their lives from one day to the next, and where was God?

That's what I was thinking about sitting on this subway train. I must have looked depressed and the man across the aisle he says, "So what's going on?" "Nothing is going on," I say because that's how I felt. Nothing is getting better. Everything is getting worse. There's no help, there's nothing worth doing. I think I'll just huddle up in the subway train without so much as lifting a prayer to the heavens. I'm done.

Then the subway train came to a stop, the man stood up. "Make it happen," he says to me. "Make it happen."

It wasn't an earthquake or a fire. This wasn't a blowing wind that swept me up ... just a man on a subway who changed my whole life. That voice dashed my assumptions and opened my eyes.

It happened to Elijah that way.

Hope was lost.

He was lost, but God tracked him down and asked: "What are you doing here, Elijah?"

He answered, "I have been very zealous for the Lord, the God of hosts; for the Israelites have forsaken your covenant, thrown down your altars, and killed your prophets by the sword. I alone am left, and they are seeking my life to take it away."

Did you hear that? "I alone am left," he said.

That's quite an assumption, so the Lord said to him, "Go! Return on your way, [for there are] seven thousand in Israel ... all the knees that have not bowed to Baal."

I'm afraid that sometimes we give up too easily.

We assume it's over when the story has only begun; for it is when hope seems to be lost that God speaks one last word that changes everything.

We forget, we assume, we despair, but there it was in Romans: "The word is near you, on your lips and in your heart," and that Word spoke to Elijah, that Word spoke to me, that Word is alive and well here and now finding us, redeeming us, filling us up – and sending us out.

"Make it happen," the man said to me.

"Go back to Israel," God said to Elijah.

And "How beautiful are the feet of those who bring good news," Paul says to us today.

"How are they to call on one in whom they have not believed? And how are they to believe in one of whom they have not heard? And how are they to hear without someone to proclaim him? And how are they to proclaim him unless they are sent?"

Once God tracks us down and speaks to us, we are sent right out to speak to the world. But what will we say? Will we say it right? Will they listen?

This is my third Sunday here. The first two Sundays I was nervous. Now I'm self-conscious, because I watched myself the other day. I've always tried to listen to myself to hear whether I'm speaking too fast or mumbling. But watching myself might do more harm than good, because Melissa up there in the sound booth who video tapes this worship service has this one camera angle that's like right on a bald spot that I didn't even know was there.

It's true.

And now as I watch myself preach, I can also see who in the choir is really listening and who is just making notes on their music. Who's sleeping. I couldn't see anybody sleeping, but it is fun to watch you guys. Jim Goodlet's face made me feel like I was saying some good stuff up here, which is nice. Then there are some others who start out listening with their arms crossed but then loosen up and laugh a little, which I like seeing. Still, it's hard learning how you look and considering how you might be perceived. You might reach the assumption that nothing is happening, and no one is listening.

But it's not just our lips and what comes out of them – it's our feet.

You've heard it said that 80% of life is showing up, and I believe that's true. To show up, to try, to be present – that's most of it, and there's more Scripture to back that up. You remember what Jesus told his disciples in the Gospel of Matthew: "When they hand you over [to be tried and persecuted], do not worry about how you are to speak or what you are to say; for what you are to say will be given to you at that time." So, there's a difference between being there and not showing up assuming they won't listen.

There's a difference between showing up at a funeral wondering whether or not they'll even notice that you were there, and not showing up assuming they won't notice.

There is a difference between setting foot in the hospital room to sit by a dying friend not knowing what to say, and assuming there's no point in going.

There is a difference between getting to know a teacher by seeing her in action, and assuming education in this country is failing and teachers are the problem.

There is a difference between setting foot in Roosevelt Circle or Juarez, Mexico and seeing our neighbors face-to-face, and assuming there's nothing we can do to fight crime and poverty in our world.

And there's a difference between walking up to people who think differently and plowing into them in a silver sports car.

Yesterday it was in Charlottesville, Virginia. A protest ends in murder as a driver speeds into a crowd of people he disagrees with. Is that what God would do? Is that what God would lead anyone to do? In this world of division, hopelessness, ignorance, hatred, racism, and misinformation, Paul writes, "How beautiful are the feet." And I'll paraphrase here: "How beautiful are the feet of those who don't put their faith in assumptions, but trust that God, who finds us when we are lost and in darkness calls us out to meet our brothers and sisters who are still there."

Ours is a God who has drawn near, walked the lonesome valley with us, not looking down from heaven in times of our distress, but coming as near to us to know all our joy and all our pain, taking human form to know us rather than make assumptions about who we are. So, go and do likewise. Go to them. Go to them and do not assume that you already know who they are. Do not assume that they already know what you must bring, and do not worry about what you will say – for it's not the mouth, nor the words, but the feet.

Beautiful are the feet.

Amen.

The Path of Totality
Isaiah 56:1, 6-8 and Romans 11:1-2a, 29-32

You might have seen a picture of me that I posted on Facebook a couple weeks ago. Mike Clotfelter brought it by and maybe you saw it if you're into Facebook and have seen our church's Facebook page. It's a picture of me and Matt Buchanan and some other guys when we were in High School. We had a band, though not everyone would call it that. I use the word "band" loosely. We sort of made music, and seeing this picture was affirmation of something that I already knew: that it's going to be a little different being a pastor in a church where people remember what I was like in High School.

Since being here I've been overjoyed to shake hands with old Sunday School teachers – all these people who did their best to nurture me in the faith. On my first Sunday here, four weeks ago now, one of the first people I saw was Nate Marini. All I could think of when I saw him was, "I hope you can forgive me."

I've seen Bob and Vivian Stephens. She taught us music during Sunday School and I know that I can sing every song in that songbook verbatim. They're all right here in my heart, and that's saying something, because back then I wasn't in a place where I was paying that close of attention.

It's a lesson in forgiveness being here. Forgiveness, acceptance, a lesson in love – all of that. And I say this because the verse that people have been quoting to me since announcing this move away from Tennessee and back to the church I grew up in has been Luke 4:24: "Truly I tell you, no prophet is accepted in the prophet's hometown."

It can be a scary thing coming home, but then there are these moments. Last Thursday morning when Ken Farrar tells a group of 100 or so at a men's Bible Study that he was my 7th grade Sunday School teacher. And while he had the chance, he left out the details about any misadventures or misbehavior.

It's a gift to be back here. It's a gift to come home. And I say a gift, because I know better than to take this for granted. Not everyone feels like they can ever go back home. It is a gift to know that we are welcomed back.

On the other hand, in fear, sometimes when we think of God, some of us imagine the great scorekeeper who's been keeping track of what we've done and what we shouldn't have done. One who has been keeping track of debts owed and wrongs to right, but the counter to this image is the father in the parable of the Prodigal Son. You know this one well. A son goes away,

43

squanders his inheritance on loose living, and in desperation he returns home, just hoping that his father will allow him to come and work as one of his hired hands.

He's surprised then that his father rushes out the door to meet him, and before he's so much as apologized, he's been embraced by the grace and forgiveness of a parent who is just so thankful to have his son come back home. This is God – a Father longing for a relationship restored.

That's a beautiful image, and I believe this image is important.

I prayed something similar this past week. A friend named Marcy Lay, the Music Director at the church I served in Columbia, Tennessee, gave me a prayer book called *The Valley of Vision*. Marcy is the kind of person who will really wear out a prayer book. She gave me this book, and with the book came a note saying that she'd be praying for me as I began my ministry here, and when Marcy says she'll pray for you she means it. That's a real blessing.

One morning this week I prayed a prayer from that book with this phrase, which struck me as timely:

O Lord, show me what sins hide Thee from me
And eclipse thy love.

That's poetic, isn't it? Prayer books are good this way. The book of Psalms is good this way. The words prayed by others become personal, because they finally give voice to the deep feelings of our own hearts. Plus, these words are way more poetic than any that I could dream up, yet they articulate something that I've personally felt – that the truly detrimental result of my sin isn't punishment so much as separation, and what God desires deeply is to remove the sin that hides God from me.

O Lord show me what sins hide Thee from me – this is a prayer for a restored relationship. This prayer is a request and acknowledgement, a prayer calling on God to remove this obstacle that stands in the way of a full, loving, relationship, and an acknowledgement that this obstacle, this road block, is of my own creation. However, what we believe about Christ is that in His death and resurrection the obstacle has been removed, forgiven, washed away in the waters of baptism, so that the Father can rush out to embrace His son.

O Lord show me what sins hide Thee from me – this is a good prayer of confession that must be followed with a celebration. Hearing these words inspires our rejoicing in the truth that what the Presbyterian *Book of Common Worship* says is true: "The mercy of the Lord is from everlasting to everlasting and in the name of Jesus Christ we are forgiven." But if you'll remember, while the Prodigal Son was embraced by his father, the Prodigal's brother stood smugly by.

That's a horrible place to be.

Shouldn't we all long for the day when God's love would no more be eclipsed for anyone?

And speaking of eclipse, apparently something is happening with the sun and the moon tomorrow. I don't know if you've heard anything about it.

Sara and I plan to take our girls out of school early so that we can all be outside together wearing our ridiculous glasses to witness this moment of darkness in the middle of the day. The moon blocking the sun's rays just as sin might block God's love.

Even though we are not quite in "The Path of Totality", which is without a doubt the coolest phrase I've ever heard to describe anything ... even though we don't live exactly on that slice of the earth that will experience total eclipse, what I will now be thinking about as the moon blocks the light from the sun are the ways that my sin can hide me from God ... ways that I might be tempted to hide from a loving Father. In truth, this loving God sent his son to the earth to push the moon aside so that we might all bask in the warmth of God's wonderful love.

That's grace. That's forgiveness.

But sometimes it is those of us who have received a gift that are the worst about passing it on. That's why Paul lectures the Christians in Rome about the Jews, saying, "I ask, then, has God rejected his people? By no means! For the gifts and calling of God are irrevocable. [And] just as you were once disobedient to God but have now received mercy... so they have now been disobedient in order that...they may now receive mercy from you."

Now that's big. It's a big warning to any of us who are tempted to act like the Prodigal's brother. Paul still asks, "How can you, who have now received mercy, withhold mercy?"

The issue Paul is addressing here is both historic and timeless. In those days, there was the issue of understanding how the Jewish people could be both waiting for a Messiah while rejecting Him once he showed up. Many Christians felt about those Jews the way we feel about any and all the people who left or rejected us. "They can just sleep in the bed that they've made for themselves," some say. But, I ask, "How can I, as one who has received mercy, deny mercy to someone else?"

That's the word that Paul has for us today – a reminder of how this grace thing works – a lesson on what forgiveness is – and a call to remember that we are not here because we are perfect, because we are holy, because we are better than anyone else. No. What unifies us who are here is that we know that we are sinners in need of forgiveness ... that we have received such forgiveness from a merciful Savior who pushed the moon aside so that we might bask in the love of God.

Therefore, it's always important to remember that we must pass on the grace that we've received, because the world is misunderstanding who we are and what we believe, calling us judgmental and self-righteous. Some call us Christians because sometimes we are. But as the people of God, when we turn our backs and suspend grace to those who need it, we preach a gospel of condemnation to a people still walking in darkness. That's unacceptable, isn't it? Especially when you consider what the Prophet Isaiah said: "Thus, says the Lord God, who gathers the outcasts of Israel, I will gather others to them besides those already gathered, even foreigners and eunuchs."

Our expectation must be that God is about the work of gathering more and more and more, rather than fencing out and drawing lines and building walls to keep so many out.

We must be about gathering and not excluding.

We must be about welcoming and not turning our backs.

We must be about grace and love and forgiveness rather than debts and failings and shortcomings because returning home takes courage – far too much courage to greet the Prodigal Son with anything other than the grace that we ourselves received.

As our public discourse becomes harsher, as our country becomes more divided and more self-righteous, the goal must be to move closer to "the path of civility" as the Marietta Daily Journal put it just this morning, moving ever further away from the path of total and complete eclipse blocking the redeeming rays of God's love and mercy.

It's not too late for the Neo-Nazi to see the light, but he must realize that he is no more a child of God than the Jew.

It's not too late for the Klansman to bask in the light of love, but he must not be so bold as to deny such love to his brother with a different shade of skin.

And the liberals must remember this as they march, recognizing that just because they believe they have some good solutions to old problems, if it's only the liberals who are going to make it to the Promised Land leaving everyone else out then I'm not sure I'm very interested in going.

No one has all the answers. And just as God is about the work of gathering all people together, so must we.

We can't be like Jonah, disappointed that the Ninevites repent and are reconciled to God. The hatred that infects this nation is the enemy – not the people who embody the hatred – because God wants them back too.

God is about removing the stumbling block – pushing whatever it is that separates us from His love out of the way, so we must be about the work of pushing away what divides us – be that hatred, fear, or self-righteous judgment.

The goal must be staying together, passing on the same mercy that we have received rather than standing in judgment.

We must remember that salvation is good and joyful. We've heard too much judgment and guilt, haven't we?

I remember too well one summer when I was a counselor at Camp Cherokee.

The preacher gave his talk to this group of young campers. It was all about the Cross and the suffering of our Lord. He told them about the crown and how when they put the crown of thorns on His head blood dripped down the sides of his face.

"But that's not what killed him children," the preacher said.

"Then they whipped him, and they whipped him to within an inch of his life."

"But that's not what killed him children, because then they took these big rusty nails, and they pounded those nails into his hands, but even that's not what finally killed him children. Do you know what finally killed him?"

A young man, 9 or 10, lifted his voice and he asked, "Was its tetanus?"

That young man reminded me to laugh, and that's good because salvation is Good News.

Forgiveness is Good News.

Grace is Good News.

Too good for the people who have received it to cover it up with shame, fear, or judgment.

Amen.

One Body
Exodus 1:8 – 2:10 and Romans 12:1-8

It's been many years since I've been in Holland Hall, but when I'm in here I still think of all these memories, especially those afternoons when we'd come here to play basketball – so excited as 15 and 16-year-olds can be about basketball. But sometimes we'd hit that door only to realize that Scottish dancing or something else was already happening in here and we'd have to go somewhere else to play.

I remember complaining to someone about it. Maybe it was Paul Sherwood who used to schedule which group had which room and at which time, and he told me that with a church this big we have to work together – we have to use a calendar and reserve our rooms, and no, I couldn't just play basketball whenever I wanted.

That's the reality of life in community.

You can't just play basketball whenever you want. You must think of others. You must plan. You must be mindful of what everyone else is doing.

So, Paul tells the church in Rome that we must think of ourselves, not as individuals, but as part of something bigger – as a part of the body of Christ: "For as in one body we have many members, and not all the members have the same function, so we, who are many, are one body in Christ, and individually we are members one of another."

That makes sense when you think of a room like this. We have to be aware that there are many members but one body and we have to work together. We have to schedule, we have to be mindful, not just of what we want to do and when we want to play basketball, but of how we fit into the whole.

That's how it is in a church, that's how it is in a family, that's how it is in a marriage, that's how it is in friendship, but today it seems to me that this way of thinking is no longer considered to be very American.

Today, a lot of kids don't need a basketball court like this one, because they have their own in their driveway that they can play on whenever they want. There's a danger in that. There's a danger in the ability to do what you want when you want, because you may have the freedom to shoot basketball whenever you choose, but you'll almost always play alone.

We were not meant to play alone, and so I worry about our society. I worry about what it is doing to us to have these freedoms that we have, this wealth that provides us two cars per household so we don't have to car pool because we can just drive ourselves. There's a danger in that, because if we can do most everything that we want to do when we want to do it, we start to think of independence as a virtue, and of course it is, but we Christians should know better than to think of ourselves and our success as independent of the work of others.

So, it is in our First Scripture Lesson from the book of Exodus.

Certainly, you know whom this story is about. The heading of chapter two tells you everything you need to know. It's the story of the birth and youth of Moses. But notice that Moses wasn't mentioned in our reading for today – he's not given a name until verse 10. This story isn't really his story yet – the first two chapters of Exodus is the story of strong women whose names have not been forgotten.

The heroes of this story are Shiphrah and Puah. The king of Egypt said to them, "When you act as midwives to the Hebrew women, and see them on the birth stool, if it is a boy, kill him; but if it is a girl, she shall live."

Perhaps Pharaoh was so foolish about power, believing that only a man would rebel against him, toppling him from his throne, but here he underestimated two midwives who saved the lives of innumerable boys, saying to Pharaoh, "the Hebrew women are not like the Egyptian women; for they are vigorous and give birth before the midwife comes to them."

This is strength. And these are two women whom Moses depended upon.

These two are named in chapter one of Exodus, because these two women, Shiphrah and Puah, matter. Without their faith in God, Moses would have been killed at birth.

More than that, from their story we understand that Moses was not the first to defy Pharaoh's orders. He was not the first to stand before the most powerful man in the land without cowering. These two women went before him, defying Pharaoh's power, refusing to follow his orders, finding a means to execute justice in a time of terror and fear.

But their names might have been forgotten. Moses is the name that we remember today. He is the one who seems the most important, as it is his function as liberator of the Israelites, bringer of the 10 Commandments, and as guide into the Promised Land that has been valued by generations of the faithful over these two who serve as his crafty and brave midwives.

When we recall the names Shiphrah and Puah, we can arrive at two conclusions:

1. The successful, the heroic, the rich and famous, even our most admired leaders – they are always dependent on others.
2. While we are commonly tempted to value some roles in life more than others, we may be failing to see reality for what it is.

Paul said it like this: "For by the grace given to me I say to everyone among you not to think of yourself more highly than you ought to think, but to think with sober judgment" – for we have gifts that differ according to the talents given to us: prophecy, ministry, teaching ... but may the exhorter remember that without the musician there is no worship, without the printer there is no bulletin, without the person who knows how to operate the projector there are no words on the screen – without the one who gives in generosity there is no church, without the deacon there is no structure, without the elder there is no leadership – without you there is no me and without God there is no grace. We are not independent, but completely and utterly dependent ... individually, we are members one of another.

Yet there are those of us who are forgotten. Scores of people may know the name of a celebrity, but what about her mother or housekeepers or agents.

Many in our world live their lives disconnected from reality, ungrateful to those who hold them up. A pastor I know, Rev. Bill Williamson, used to say, "There are some people who were born on third but think that they're there because they hit a triple." So it might be that a well born goes his whole life believing that he deserves privilege, that the entitled believes it is his right to receive gifts and handouts, that a 15-year-old boy gets upset when the basketball court is being used for Scottish dancing.

For some, life is easier, and blessings overflow. And should they ever ask why, we really should pity those who reach the conclusion that they deserve what they have been given.

Paul urges you not to think of yourself more highly than you ought to think, as those who fall into positions of power, prestige, and privilege without recognizing how they got there miss out on the opportunity to be thankful.

Tina Fey is not a notoriously religious woman. She's a celebrity, a comedian, but in her book titled *Bossy Pants* she included a prayer titled "The Mother's Prayer for Her Daughter".

The prayer begins, "First, Lord: No tattoos," and it ends with this:

And should she choose to be a Mother one day, be my eyes, Lord, that I may see her, lying on a blanket on the floor at 4:50 AM, all-at-once exhausted, bored, and in love with the little creature whose poop is leaking up its back. My mother did this for me once, she will realize as she cleans [who knows what] off her baby's neck. My mother did this for me.[1]

For lucky children, there is a mother.

For Moses, there were two incredible brave women.

Without these women, there might be no Moses – so who can say that one gift is better than another.

For each of us there may be special supporting members from the body of Christ – some whose names you remember, while the memory of others has faded. There are generations of faithful, those who witnessed firsthand the mighty acts of God all the way to the forefathers and foremothers of this church who gave us a place to hear the Good News and be saved. We are the recipients of their legacy. Give thanks for them all, because without them there is no you – and honor their legacy by remembering that independence is an illusion, for we are all dependent on one another – and without interdependence there is no us.

But we live in this world where so many want to have their own basketball court.

If God were our Kindergarten teacher, I believe He might give us all that harsh mark of "doesn't play well with others."

And what's worse, we're getting used to it.

The constant bickering on the opinion page of the paper and the soapbox of Facebook is starting to feel normal. We have forgotten what it means to live together in this world. We study politics while losing sight of community, and you can see it because we are growing used to life on our own couches,

---

[1] Tina Fey, *Bossy pants* (New York: Little, Brown and Company, 2011) 263.

watching the news channel that we agree with, forgetting how to interact with the person who lives next door doing nearly the exact same thing.

A room like this then is precious, for our world is no different than this Holland Hall where we must respect the fact that many people are working together, reserving space, racing pinewood derby cars one minute and Scottish dancing the next. There should be availability for all of us – but there is no room for selfishness that thinks only of "what I want and need", and there is no more room for arrogance – for we, who are many, are one body in Christ.

I saw it plainly, riding in a funeral procession. We passed the Havoline Express Lube on the corner of Whitlock and Polk Street. As we passed, the men and women working there stopped what they were doing, rushed to the street, and placed their hats over their hearts. It was a vision of community – and to me, it was a preview of the Kingdom of God.

Amen.

He Did What He Meant to Do
Jeremiah 15:15-21 and Romans 12:9-21

Last Thursday I faced a sort of moral dilemma.

Last Friday night I faced one too – Martha Goodlet asked me whether a preacher should be cheering for the Blue Devils when they're playing Holy Trinity, but I want to talk about the moral dilemma from last Thursday.

I blocked off a small part of my morning to go to the chiropractor. I've found that chiropractic really helps with all kinds of aches and pains, especially my migraine headaches. I have this wonderful new chiropractor that you know – Dr. Janet Lewis. I didn't have an appointment. I just hoped the wait wouldn't be too long, and I blocked off this time to slip in.

However, it was 8:30, and everyone else was trying to slip in – or, everyone else had made an appointment like a respectable patient. The waiting room was full, so I asked the receptionist how long she thought the wait would be. She said, "not too long, 15 or 20 minutes." But my car was at the mechanic, and Sara needed her car back that I was driving, so I told the receptionist that I would come back later.

Now the moral dilemma.

Kelly Dewar keeps up with my schedule.

She sees when I block off time for the chiropractor and doesn't plan any meetings for me during those times. It's wonderful the order she brings to my life, but when I get back to the church, I'm thinking, what if Kelly asks me, "How was the chiropractor?" What am I going to say, since now I didn't even go?

I blocked off time to go to the chiropractor, not to drive in the car for 30 minutes. That's not something I would ever schedule.

So, what I mean here is this – what do you call it if you don't do the thing that you meant to do?

Or to think in terms of faith – what do you call a person who says he believes but never puts that belief into action? Who never does the thing he meant to do? Is there such a thing as a non-practicing Christian?

I had lunch with Dr. Sam Matthews this week. He's the Senior Pastor over at First United Methodist Church. We were at the Country Club and he pointed out this table in the corner. He said, "You see those ladies? That's the No Sew Club."

"What is the No Sew Club?" I asked.

He told me "They used to sew but now they don't, which is like a lot of my church members – they're in the No Church Club – they used to come and now they don't."

What do you call it if you only used to do something?

Or, what do you call it if you never did? You only meant to?

Something that Paul brings to light today in this lesson from the 12th Chapter of his letter to the church in Rome is that Christianity is not a noun but a verb – when you stop being a Christian, when you stop living as a Christian, are you really a Christian any longer?

These words are the perfect benediction, because they send us out into the world to live our faith: "Let love be genuine; hate what is evil, hold fast to what is good."

You've heard these words before.

As I've settled into my office upstairs, I've opened the main drawer and there they are: "Go forth into the world in peace. Be of good courage. Hold fast to that which is true. Render to no one evil for evil. Strengthen the faint hearted" – you know these words because Dr. Jim Speed sent us all out into the world to live them every Sunday.

Every Sunday he preached here he reminded us as Paul does. He reminded us that we must live our faith.

And it looks funny if we don't.

As I mentioned before, my car has been in the shop. Mary Margaret Doyle sent me to see a man named Gary at the Jett Shell on Roswell Road, and he told me that if I mention him in the sermon, he'll give me a 25% discount.

I'm just kidding about that. But he did give me a ride back to the church after I dropped off the car, which was wonderful. And this guy – he's in a book club with John Knox, he's been in the mechanic business for years, and he's a

A Door Keeper in the House of the Lord

grandfather. He's a wonderful person and listen to this – his grandfather was a Baptist preacher.

Gary the mechanic's grandfather was bi-vocational, meaning that he worked in the mill up in North Georgia during the week and preached all around on Sundays. Gary cherishes his childhood memories of riding the circuit with his grandfather, hearing him preach as he traveled to the different churches.

His grandfather, a seasoned preacher, told young Gary the story of the most memorable funeral he ever officiated. As he entered the sanctuary, he could smell the flowers before he saw them. There were more flower arrangements than he had ever seen before. The chancel was covered. He could barely make his way to the pulpit. Obviously, this was a well-loved woman who had died. You could see it.

But the last song of the service was that old Gospel Song: Just One Rose Will Do.

The soloist sang, among all those flowers:

When time shall come for my leaving,
When I bid you adieu;
Don't spend your money for flowers,
Just one rose will do.

And yet the chancel, the pulpit, the whole room was covered in flowers.

What do you do with that?

What do you call it if you don't do the thing that you meant to do?

Can you sing the words without living them?

Can you believe in the Lord Jesus without following him?

Can you be a Christian without living out this faith?

That's what got me about my brother Joel Osteen this week.

I call him brother, but I love this church better than his.

I'm a little jealous of his hair, and while we are both preaching the same Gospel, what does it say about the whole Church if we declare a message of extending

56

hospitality to strangers but the doors to our church are reluctant to open in the time of disaster and flood?

Maybe you heard that eventually the doors to his church did open — that after three days the doors to that church opened to welcome in those who had lost their homes to the flood waters, and I don't know the whole story. I can't be self-righteous here, but it did strike me as odd that the Oscar Blues, Miller-Coors, and Anheuser-Bush breweries immediately shifted production from canned beer to canned water while the church took three days to open her doors.

What do you do with that?

We all must remember that for some people - the only Gospel they will ever hear is the one that we live through our actions.

When our doors are closed, they hear a Gospel of Condemnation.

When our hearts are closed, they hear a Gospel of Rejection.

When our noses are upturned and our chests inflated, they hear a Gospel of Favoritism.

But when we open our arms wide in forgiveness and reconciliation, they hear the true Gospel of our Lord Jesus Christ.

We must live our faith.

Christianity is about what we believe in our minds and carry in our hearts. The Prophet Jeremiah didn't just carry around a Bible — he ate the pages and lived the words.

So, we also must live what we believe, and what we believe is this:

That our Lord Jesus Christ came to the earth.

And when he did, he loved sinners.

He ate with outcasts.

He treasured children.

He forgave sins.

He lifted broken women up from a society that had objectified them.

He empowered fishermen to preach the most important message this world has ever heard.

And He so lived what He believed, that as the great act of love to human kind He gave his life so that you and I might know our worth in the eyes of God.

He did what He meant to do.

And what does He ask of you?

I'll say it again – not as Paul wrote it in Romans chapter 12, but as the pastor whom I grew up with said every Sunday:

Go Forth into the world in peace.
Be of good courage.
Hold fast to that which is true.
Render to no one evil for evil.
Strengthen the fainthearted.
Support the weak.
Help the afflicted.
Honor all.
Love and serve the Lord, rejoicing in the Holy Spirit.
And the grace of the Lord Jesus Christ, the love of God the Father, and the fellowship of the Holy Spirit be with you all.
Amen.

Our Heritage of Love
Ezekiel 33:7-11 and Romans 13:8-14

Today is really something, isn't it?

Never in my life have I worn a kilt. This is a new experience, and up until this point, the most I had ever done to celebrate my Scotts-Irish Heritage is to use Irish Spring Soap; eat at a little dining establishment founded by a couple of Scottish brothers called McDonalds.

This is a special day. A day like this is a gift, because celebrating who we are and where we came from can be joyful and life giving. But celebrating heritage today can also get a little dicey.

Just this word: Heritage. Considering headlines in the past few months, that word has been and will continue to be contentious, especially if you are a white-southerner. So for me, this has been another year of wondering how to celebrate heritage.

When it comes to heritage, I am often wondering, how can we, without hurting our neighbor, be proud of who we are and where we came from?

That's a question I've been asking for a long time. I remember being on the 8th Grade trip to Washington D.C. when I was a student at Marietta Middle School. A group of us were gathered around a display case full of Rebel Flag patches. I bought one, used the hotel sowing kit to sloppily attach it to my jacket, which seemed like a pretty cool way to celebrate my southern roots, until some of my African-American classmates noticed it. The hurt on their faces is something I'll never forget.

What do we do with heritage?

Some say, especially in reference to the Rebel Flag, that it's heritage, not hate, but if it feels like hate to my neighbor, I won't celebrate it.

Simply put, that's Paul's message to us today – we worry over heritage wanting to celebrate what is near and dear to our hearts – but it must not be only our hearts that we are mindful of, for any commandment is summed up in this word: Love your neighbor as yourself.

Still, there are genes that make up my body that urge me to celebrate in a loving way.

There is a blood flowing through my veins.

I am from a place that makes up my heritage. There's no denying that — I face it every time we go to the beach because I turn bright red in five minutes while my wife and children turn a gorgeous shade of brown.

I also feel it when watching a movie like *Braveheart* — that these people are my people. This is some of where I came from, and today, what's special about today, is that today I'm invited to wear a kilt and to be proud, and isn't that wonderful?

It's so wonderful that I understand the Episcopalians are wanting to have their own Kirkin' of the Tartan, even though that wouldn't make any sense.

In fact, thinking of how their tradition emerged from England just as ours has strong roots in Scotland, what should really happen is next year we should all paint our faces blue and stand in their parking lot yelling: "You may take our lives, but you'll never take our freedom!"

And maybe that's back to the problem with heritage:

- You can't talk about bagpipes without thinking about how they were once outlawed, and who outlawed them.
- You can't think about Scotts-Irish immigrants without thinking about how they faced such hardship, fled to escape it, only to find it again once they set foot on these shores.
- You can't talk about being from the South without thinking about slavery and war and discrimination, for as we go back in history, as we talk about heritage, we have to be careful because when we go back into history it takes about five minutes to find something that one group did to another, the scars of which are still all around us.

Here we are in Cobb County, where the Cherokee People were removed.

Where a Jewish man was falsely accused of a crime and was lynched.

Where a war was fought, and people died as the institution of slavery hung in the balance.

When it comes to heritage, looking back on the past, it's hard not to keep score. It's hard not to keep track of who has been wronged, who has a debt to pay, who has blood on their hands, for in so many ways the story of human history is an account of one group of people, one culture, doing their best to lift themselves up while pushing the others down — so heritage gets tricky.

However, as Christians, our heritage is not just a story of what was done or not done by our ancestors.

Ours is not just a story of who is best and brightest, whose family has been here the longest and who's blood is the bluest. For on a day like today, the point is not that Tartans were brought into this Great Hall in a grand procession, but that here at the chancel those tartans were blessed by God.

So, yes — we have some trouble when it comes to celebrating heritage, but let us be grateful for a day like today, when we are invited, all of us, to celebrate who we are, while claiming the truth of the Gospel — that truly, while we cannot be proud of all that our forefathers and foremothers have done, today we bow before the God who loves us all and calls us all his children.

Therefore, what we must celebrate today is not only the legacy of greatness, struggle, hardship, and glory. Not a heritage of prejudice, racism, genocide, and slavery. Instead, what we celebrate today is that despite our sinfulness, we are all the children of God.

That's what we remember at Pentecost too. I'm sure you remember how after the Lord ascended into heaven, the disciples gathered in Jerusalem and the Holy Spirit came to them like a mighty wind, giving each of them the gifts of tongues, so that every inhabitant of the Holy City heard God speaking to them in their own native languages.

These weren't perfect people. Among them was Thomas who doubted, Peter who denied Him — in some way or another, like us they had all done things that they were ashamed of. Still, God worked through them. And it's not that the inhabitants of Jerusalem were all able to speak the same language — no — they all heard God speak to them in their Mother Tongue, and that's different.

You remember that great quote from the first female governor of Texas, Miriam Ferguson: "If English was good enough for Jesus, it's good enough for Texas school children."

There's a problem with that statement.

The problem is that Jesus, while we all like to make him look like us, was a Palestinian Jew. He spoke their language. His hair and his skin reflected the particularities of his native people, and when he traveled around people made fun of how he talked and what he ate, just as people up in Tennessee thought it was funny that I consider boiled peanuts a delicacy.

And they are! But as we consider heritage, let me tell you something interesting about them – the peanut was first domesticated in South America. When the Spanish arrived there 500 years ago, they took it worldwide, but it truly flourished in West Africa. Some have claimed that the ancestor of the peanut that makes up the contents of your jar of JIFF was smuggled in the pocket of a West African Slave over the Atlantic Ocean.

But not only that, it was not until former slave, George Washington Carver developed new growing techniques as well as hundreds of recipes for it that there was much agricultural production of the peanut in the South by white farmers. So, without the South Americans, the Spanish, the West Africans, and a former slave, there is no peanut farming President Jimmy Carter, and there is no redneck boiling peanuts on the side of the North Georgia back-road.

We get so torn up about race and culture – heritage – but are we not indebted to each other?

Are we not far more entwined than we are separate?

And are we not above all, not vindicated nor condemned for our part, but rather, indebted to God who works through us despite our imperfections.

Our history books are full of great deeds and tragic mistakes, a mixed bag of heroes and villains, and we Christians who pray, "forgive us our debts as we forgive our debtors" must take seriously those words – for we all stand before God condemned, but we have received a grace that we cannot deserve.

"How then can we withhold such grace from our neighbors?" – that's what Paul asks. "Owe no one anything, except to love one another," he says. Still, there are those of us who are tempted to keep score and to puff ourselves up as Ezekiel did. This prophet had been given a message to preach to the people, but he only wanted some of them to hear it and be saved. So, God had to correct him just as God must correct us: "As I live, says the Lord God, I have no pleasure in the death of the wicked, but that the wicked turn from their ways and live."

As I look at our world today, I worry that too few are ready for that kind of message.

Are we ready for a God who wants to save everybody regardless of native language, skin color, or nationality?

Are we ready for the God that Paul testifies to? In whose sight there is no Jew, nor Greek, no slave nor free, no male and female?

The Gospel lays it on our culture heavy.

So many of us are ready to celebrate who we are and where we came from regardless of how it makes our neighbors feel.

So many of us are only willing to treat the people who look like us and talk like us as equals, while pushing those who act a little different to the margins.

That's why Paul must remind us of those radical words of the Lord Jesus Christ: "Love your neighbor as yourself."

And that's a hard thing to do…especially during college football season.

You watch the crowds and listen to what they say. You must wonder if Georgia fans hate Florida fans this much, then how are we ever going to get along with people who really are different? How are we ever going to get along with those to whom we have done harm and with those who have done harm to us?

Tomorrow we remember that horrible day when airplanes were used as weapons by men who called us infidels, and we'll remember all the bloodshed in the wars that have followed. But may the blood shed on our sanctuary floor so many years ago help us to remember something else — that while the war raged on Kennesaw Mountain, in this place there was healing.

And we have been called on to be a place of healing again.

Last week a Nursing Home in Savannah, Georgia called the church looking for a place of refuge during the hurricane. They needed us to be their plan B. They had a place to go in Augusta, Georgia, but if the hurricane went that way, they'd need a safe place to be further away from the storm.

The Session met. Rev. Joe Brice, Martie Moore, and Andy Tattnall led the charge, all believing that what Joe Brice said was true: "If this church has already been a hospital once, we can be a nursing home too."

Of course, now, it maybe it we who are evacuating to them, but the Session amazed me in discussing all of this, because opening our doors this way to a bunch of people we don't even know is a radical thing to do.

There's a part of our heritage that makes us suspicious of people who don't look like us or talk like us, who "aren't from around here." But we, who know that we are sinners, know that we stand as debtors before the God of Grace who has redeemed us.

What is required then, is that we see our neighbors, not in light of what might be gained from them or what they might take away, not in light of what they've done to deserve our help or not deserve it, but to see them only in light of what we might give them, acknowledging the truth — that by God we have been given far more than we deserve, so we must pass our blessings on.

"Let us then lay aside the works of darkness and put on the armor of light; let us live honorably as in the day, not in reveling and drunkenness, not in debauchery and licentiousness [or any of the other ways that we humans have for treating our neighbors like objects of physical pleasure], not in quarreling and jealousy [for are we not all God's children?]."

Instead of rivalry and war, let us love on another.

For it is in loving one another that we so truly celebrate our heritage... not our heritage of hate, but our heritage of love.

Amen.

Am I in the Place of God?
Genesis 50:15-21 and Romans 14:1-12

To me, one of the most powerful lessons from our Lord Jesus Christ is the one he taught us when a woman was caught in adultery.

You know this one well.

A woman! We don't know how old she was. We don't know what she looked like. There are few details, so we don't know whether she was caught in the act or if this punishment has come after the fact. Nor do we know where her partner in crime was in this moment of condemnation. But what I imagine, without really knowing, is that she was alone, cowering as a crowd of self-righteous men gathered around her, stones in their hands.

The Lord kneeled next to her, wrote something in the dirt with his finger, and said with conviction but to no one in particular, "Let he who is without sin, cast the first stone."

This is a radical Word, and herein lies a radical lesson for all of us who would stand in judgment of our sister, for He doesn't argue for her innocence. What He argues for is for us to recognize our guilt.

That's important to do. And in a way, here at this church, we reinforce such a lesson every Sunday. Today like every Sunday when we first gathered here to worship God, we began by confessing our sins – recognizing our guilt – which is important to do.

I wrote the prayer of confession that we used today. You all prayed this prayer together, out loud, for everyone to hear. So now I can assume that you, like me, have trouble with forgiving your neighbor, but you have been forgiven for this shortfall because you made the confession with me.

You might have just been following along with what everyone else was doing when you read those words, but I'm going to call it a confession because you prayed the words: "The Lord does not deal with us according to our sins, nor repay us according to our iniquities, but I retain the sins of my neighbor, refusing to let go."

Maybe now you'll think twice before reading along with what's printed in the bulletin. Maybe you didn't realize I was listening for a confession, but that's exactly the point of the prayer.

What is required of us, we who gather here to worship, is so like what is required of those who gather for Alcoholics Anonymous meetings. The first step in AA is: "We admitted we were powerless over alcohol, that our lives had become unmanageable." And this first step towards sobriety is the same as the first step towards salvation – what's required is not innocence, but confession. We admitted we were sinners in need of a savior, and we found one in Jesus Christ. We aren't here because we're innocent. We aren't here because we're good.

No, what qualifies our membership here is a confession of sin, an acknowledgement of our need for a savior, and a willingness to admit that we cannot save ourselves.

The Good News for our world full of people struggling to save themselves is that we don't have to. The Good News is that Jesus Christ died on the cross to save sinners, but the problem that Paul addresses for us today is that while we may rationally know and accept the truth of that statement in our hearts, we are too often like those men with stones in their hands, as though not being guilty today were the same as being innocent.

Sometimes, we act like vegetarians.

Not the kind who just don't eat meat – I'm talking about the ones who don't eat meat and like to make sure and tell you about it.

Did you hear the one about the vegetarian who walked into a bar?

In 15 minutes, he had told everybody. That's the whole joke (the early service didn't get it either).

Paul says it like this: "Some believe in eating anything, while the weak eat only vegetables. Those who eat must not despise those who abstain, and those who abstain must not pass judgment on those who eat; for God has welcomed them."

See the point?

The point is not that vegetarians should eat meat. They're just fine, and in fact, when you consider how our rainforests are so rapidly being depleted, not just by deforestation, but also to make room for more and more grazing land for beef cattle, we carnivores who enjoy breathing would do well to thank a vegetarian occasionally.

Instead, we meat-eaters make fun of them.

I saw a t-shirt for sale in a BBQ restaurant one time that said, "Vegetarian is the Cherokee word for he who can't hunt." That's not nice – and as Paul asked, "who are you to pass judgment on servants of another?"

Paul's point here is that we all are the woman caught in adultery.

Maybe we did less and she did more, or maybe we have even more to be forgiven for than she did, but that doesn't matter. The point is – if you have been redeemed and forgiven, then stop acting like you don't need the same forgiveness that your neighbor does.

"Why do you pass judgment on your brother or sister? Or you, why do you despise your brother or sister? For we will all stand before the judgment seat of God [not the judgment seat of you or me or your daddy or your self-righteous sister] - we will stand before the judgment seat of God [and if you're judging your neighbor, then you're in the wrong seat]."

Get down from the judgment seat. That's the point. That's Paul's point.

And Paul must make this point because those who comprehend the grace of God should have no need to distract from their own guilt by pointing out the sins of their neighbor.

Christianity can't be about shaming or making someone feel guilty, but that's the practice of so many who claim to follow Christ, so Paul must make this point.

Paul knows what motivates our finger pointing. We judge when we feel judged. We make others feel insecure because we feel insecure. We withhold grace from our neighbors because we withhold grace from ourselves, which is an awful thing to do in Paul's mind for if we don't enjoy the grace that God gives, then to use his words, "Christ died for nothing."

That's Galatians 2:21: "I do not nullify the grace of God; for if justification comes through the law, then Christ died for nothing." And what does that mean?

That means that we can't save ourselves. We can't be perfect. And if we go trying to be, if we go around acting like we are, then all that suffering that Christ endured for us and for our salvation was for nothing.

We are saved by the grace of God – so don't judge yourself or your neighbor by a standard of perfection. You don't have to be perfect, because He was perfect for us.

That's Good News. And that's the kind of Good News that changes things.

Consider how it changed Joseph.

There's a picture of him on the cover of your bulletin. He's there with his brothers, and you'll notice that he's in the judgment seat on the right, but on the left he is cowering in the shadow.

If you were Joseph, then most people would say that you had a right to be judgmental. Think about what his brothers did to him. Do you remember?

They were jealous because daddy loved him the most, gave him the nicest clothes and the easiest jobs, and motivated by their jealousy they threw him down into a pit, which was better than their original plan to kill him. They then they sold him to a caravan of Ishmaelites who took him away.

The story gets worse.

I like to think that older siblings will look after the younger ones, but these guys – they sold him, told dad he had been eaten. He ended up in Egypt, then was falsely accused of a crime and ended up in prison. Any and all of these events are good justification for being angry with these brothers when they come to him now looking for help, but how could he be angry when it was these events that led Joseph to rise in power. It was in the prison that he met Pharaoh, interpreted his dreams, and became his trusted advisor.

Now, as these brothers grovel before him, on the one hand what Joseph could have seen were the big brothers who now weren't so big. But instead, what he saw were the men who were used by God to help him rise in power and status, now putting him in a place where he can save his family from starvation. So, Joseph said to them, "Do not be afraid! Am I in the place of God? Even though you intended to do harm to me, God intended it for good, in order to preserve a numerous people, as He is doing today."

Can you really get mad if everything turned out this well?

Can you hold a grudge, when God took someone's evil intentions and did something wonderful?

Would you dare stand in judgment, taking the place of God, when you know that through the grace of God life for you is good?

To quote the *Frozen* soundtrack: "Let it go."

Just let it go.

Forgive them, because you have been forgiven.

That's the lesson. And if you take it to heart, then you won't be a part of the self-righteousness that fuels so much division in our country and our world.

It's hard for me to watch the news these days.

A lot of the time current events remind me of that old Buffalo Springfield song: "Nobody's Right if Everybody's Wrong."

Just as Paul addresses this congregation all torn up over who eats meat and who doesn't, we live in a country where families divide and friendships end over who gets elected and who believes what. There are Fox News people and CNN people. Red States and Blue States. Prolife and prochoice and currently to me there's been no more helpful advice than the 1952 speech by Mississippi State Representative and Judge Noah Soggy Sweat Jr.

Addressing the contentious question of prohibition, Judge Sweat stood before the Mississippi State Legislature and said:

My friends, I had not intended to discuss this controversial subject at this time. However, I want you to know that I do not shun controversy. On the contrary, I will take a stand on any issue at any time, regardless of how fraught with controversy it might be. You have asked me how I feel about whiskey. All right, this is how I feel about whiskey:

If when you say whiskey you mean the devil's brew, the poison scourge, the bloody monster, that defiles innocence, dethrones reason, destroys the home, creates misery and poverty, yea, literally takes the bread from the mouths of little children; if you mean the evil drink that topples the Christian man and woman from the pinnacle of righteous, gracious living into the bottomless pit of degradation, and despair, and shame and helplessness, and hopelessness, then certainly I am against it.

But, if when you say whiskey you mean the oil of conversation, the philosophic wine, the ale that is consumed when good fellows get together, that puts a song in their hearts and laughter on their lips, and the warm glow of contentment in their eyes; if you mean Christmas cheer; if you mean the stimulating drink that puts the spring in the old gentlemen's step on a frosty, crispy morning; if you mean the drink which enables a man to magnify joy, and his happiness, and to forget, if only for a little while, life's great tragedies, and heartaches and sorrows; if you mean that drink, the sale of which pours into our treasuries untold millions of dollars, which are used to provide tender care for our little crippled children, our blind, our deaf, our dumb, and pitiful aged and infirm; to build highways and hospitals and schools, then certainly I am for it.

This is my stand. I will not retreat from it. I will not compromise.

We get so caught up in who is right and who is wrong – but are we not all wrong?

And is He not the only one who ever got it right?

So quickly we gather stones, but am I in the place of God? Knowing what is right and what is true?

No, I am not.

Thanks be to God, I am not.

Amen.

Part 2

Philippians

As a lectionary preacher (one who follows the Scripture passages assigned to each Sunday of the Christian year), I've grown to appreciate those times when there is an opportunity to move through a book of the Bible in a sermon series. The following is a brief series on Philippians.

The Privilege of Suffering
Jonah 3:10 – 4:11 and Philippians 1:21-30

One of my favorite TV shows of all time is *Seinfeld*. It hasn't been on for a while, but you might remember that Elaine's most notorious boyfriend was a guy named Puddy. At some point Puddy became a Christian.

Now how did she know?

He didn't tell her that he became a Christian. His behavior never changed – he was still self-centered and one-dimensional. In fact, the only reason Elaine found out about this major change in her boyfriend was that she borrowed his car and noticed that all the radio presets were set to Christian Radio, and he put a silver Jesus fish on the back.

Elaine peeled it off.

What made me think about this episode, which aired in 1998, was this week's Scripture Lessons that I just read – both lessons describe two men, both of whom would tell you that they are trying to follow God, live righteous lives, but how do you know?

How can you tell that someone is serious about following God?

The song we used to sing in choir with Mrs. Stephens during Sunday School goes like this:

"And they'll know we are Christians by our love, by our love" - not by our preset radio stations and our Jesus fish, but "by our love."

So, what do we learn about Jonah? What sermon does his life preach?

Jonah was really something.

Considering all the prophets – Isaiah, Jeremiah, Hosea, John the Baptist – all these powerful voices who cried out: "Repent! Change your ways!" - out of all of them Jonah was by far the most successful, doing the least and getting the best results.

He preached just once.

His sermon wasn't even that good. We read in Jonah chapter three that Jonah began to go into the city, going a day's walk. And he cried out: "Forty days more, and Nineveh shall be overthrown." That was his whole sermon. That's it, and yet, there in chapter 3 verse 5, "The people of Nineveh believed God; they proclaimed a fast and everyone, great and small put on sackcloth."

You don't have to be a Bible scholar to know that this never happens.

What usually happens is the prophet proclaims a message, vivid and poetic, over the course of years. Maybe, like Elijah or Elisha, he offers some convincing proof of the validity of his message – a miracle, or a healing – or maybe like Ezekiel or Hosea he lives his message by cooking his meals over cow dung and taking a prostitute for his wife, but even after such miracles or dramatic displays, what usually happens is that no one really listens to the prophet until after someone kills him.

Only Jonah preaches one sermon, one sentence long, and immediately a whole city of foreigners repents.

You would think he'd be proud, but what happens next is even more surprising than his success. That's what our First Scripture Lesson for today was – Jonah's response to the most successful prophetic career recorded in Scripture.

Following such a dramatic show of repentance he should be preparing his speech for his induction into the Prophet's Hall of Fame, but instead, "When God saw what [the Ninevites] did, how they turned from their evil ways, God changed His mind about the calamity that He had said He would bring upon them; and He did not do it. But this was very displeasing to Jonah, and he became angry."

He was so angry in fact, that he wished that he might die.

Now, in many ways, Jonah was a righteous man. His had a career in ministry – he was no dresser of sycamore trees like the Prophet Amos – this guy was a professional prophet charged with listening to God, doing what God commanded him, but even if there had been a Jesus fish on the back of the whale that he drove in on, I wonder about him, because while he doesn't steal, while he doesn't use crass language, and while he probably went to worship every Sabbath day, did he love the people he proclaimed his message to?

Isn't that really the only thing that matters?

Paul on the other hand – think about Paul.

You remember 1 Corinthians 13? You should because it's been read at every wedding in the history of weddings: "If I speak in the tongues of mortals and of angels, but do not have love, I am a noisy gong or a clanging cymbal. And if I have prophetic powers, and understand all mysteries and all knowledge, and if I have all faith, to remove mountains, but do not have love, I am nothing."

I'll add to that — even if there's a Jesus fish on the back of your car, even if you preach through the streets a one sentence sermon, even if people listen to what you say and repent from their sinfulness, if you don't have love in your heart for your neighbor, what's the point in what you're doing?

Paul has some very important things to say to the Church today, because while many in our community listen to Christian radio and buy out Hobby Lobby with all the trappings of Christianity — according to him it doesn't matter what we listen to or what we hang on our wall if we don't have love in our heart.

I like Paul for making that point. And the whole time I've been here I've been preaching from Paul's letters. I hope you don't mind.

We've just finished Romans last week. Now we're beginning four weeks of Philippians, and while I preach on Philippians Dr. Jim Speed is teaching a class on Philippians — so by the end of October we should all be Philippians experts.

Of interest when it comes to Philippians is that Paul is writing this letter from prison. This physical location matters, because you can compare where he was in body and where he was in spirit as you read this letter.

He wrote to a church that he loved, and you can hear it in his words how much he loved this congregation. He doesn't start this letter: To whom it may concern — no, he writes in verse 12: "I want you to know, beloved." That's what he called them: "Beloved."

And as you heard this passage from chapter 1 read, I'm sure you could tell that here he isn't so concerned with himself, whether he will be released, whether he will live or die, for in verse 21 we read: "For to me, living is Christ and dying is gain. If I am to live in the flesh, that means fruitful labor for me; and I do not know which I prefer. I am hard pressed between the two: my desire is to depart and be with Christ, [but if I remain] I may share abundantly in your boasting Christ Jesus when I come to you again."

Consider that love — his love for God is so deep that he has abandoned any concern for his own physical wellbeing. He has surrendered to the will of God, and he is so free from selfishness, so full of love for God's people, that you know this guy is a Christian.

Then, compare Paul, who is in prison, and Jonah, who is not.

That is a strong juxtaposition.

Paul is in prison, but he's happy.

Jonah is sitting outside, but he's miserable.

Why is that?

I believe that part of the answer comes from our *Book of Confessions*. As Presbyterians, we benefit from this beautiful legacy of faith – for generations faithful men and women have struggled to say what they believe. Most often we take advantage of this legacy by using the Apostles' Creed – we today articulate our faith by saying what they – the first Apostles - believed, and that's good, but in fact, we have a whole book full of such affirmations of faith. It's called the *Book of Confessions*.

Another confession besides the Apostles' Creed is the Westminster Confession, which begins with this question: What is the chief end of man?

The answer: "Man's chief end is to glorify God, and to enjoy him forever." That's a counter cultural thought, for in our world today, if many were to answer honestly, they might say that their chief end, their purpose, is to make as much money as they can or to gain power and to hold on to it. Some might say that their purpose is to get as many people to pay attention to them as possible. Another person might say that it is to "suck the marrow out of life" – that's from Henry David Thoreau, and it's a good one, though not the best.

When I think about the kind of people who can really rejoice, who embody joy, who are free from the self-centered misery torturing so many in our own culture, just like Jonah … when I think of such people who even in prison chains are able to keep a smile on their face, I see faithful men and women who gaze beyond their present circumstances, believing, knowing that their lives serve a greater purpose – the greatest purpose of all … to glorify God.

Consider Martin Luther King Jr., who wrote his greatest letter from the Birmingham Jail.

Or consider Nelson Mandela who said, "As I walked out the door toward the gate that would lead to my freedom, I knew if I didn't leave my bitterness and hatred behind, I'd still be in prison."

That's Jonah – still so consumed by his hatred of these Ninevites that even though he's free he's in prison, while the Apostle Paul is in prison but completely free because hatred can't hold him captive.

Stone walls do not a prison make,
Nor iron bars a cage.
Minds innocent and quiet take
That for a hermitage.
If I have freedom in my love
And in my soul am free
Angels alone that soar above
Enjoy such liberty.

I wrote that poem for Sara yesterday. No, I'm just kidding – I wish I did. That comes from the final stanza of Richard Lovelace's poem, 'To Althea, from Prison,' and in these words is the reminder that love can set you free.

The world needs to remember that.

But, to quote the Everly Brothers: Love hurts, too.

I've titled this sermon "The Privilege of Suffering".

I have trouble with sermon titles because I must come up with them on Tuesday and I often don't have a sermon written until at least Friday, but this title isn't so bad because there are those of us who know that suffering can be a gift, a privilege, especially when we suffer out of love.

Jonah isn't suffering in this way. The sun is in his eyes and he's whining about it. Don't you hate being around that kind of person? He's also suffering because he's only thinking of himself, and that's the worst!

On the other hand, Paul is suffering in body, but this is what he has to say about it: "Should you face opposition and struggle, know that [God] has graciously granted you the privilege not only of believing in Christ, but of suffering with Him as well."

When we suffer out of love for God or our neighbor, we suffer with Christ – because we know that Christ suffered out of love for you and me.

And His great suffering – He wouldn't have changed it. He wouldn't have avoided it. He went to the cross on purpose, because doing anything else would have been abandoning the people He loves and if those are the two options –

loving and suffering or abandoning us – God chooses to stay and suffer every time.

That's not unlike the love that you who are parents have for your children.

You try to give your children love, and for a while they just soak it up, but try to hold their hand when you know they're scared walking into Middle School for the first time and see what happens.

A few years down the line, you want to give them your stuff and they won't take it.

You know my grandmother told my mom for years that after her funeral, "If you dare drag my furniture out of the house for a yard sale, I'll haunt you for the rest of your life."

Love is a source of suffering – you love people and it's hard because it's like your heart is outside your chest. The people who you love also disappoint you. They hurt themselves. They do foolish things – and don't you know that our Father in heaven knows all about it.

But what did He do?

Even after death on the Cross, He rose again three days later so that He could love us more.

Love hurts, but if there's love in your heart you'll be free, even in prison.

And love shows – because even if there's a fish on your car, if you cut in front of someone and give them the bird, they'll see who you really are.

We'll go out into the world today – and may they know that we are Christians by our love, and I charge you with this for two reasons:

1. Because that's one way we glorify God, thereby living out our purpose
2. Because our creator just happened to make living out our purpose the only thing that will bring us joy and fulfillment.

So, even when it hurts, go on loving and be free.

A groom told me a story last Monday night. He was talking about his wedding day. How nervous he was about remembering his vows. There he was up in front of the church – friends and family all around – "What if I freeze and it's time to speak but nothing comes out?" he's thinking to himself.

But then the doors open. The congregation stands. And he sees his bride, the woman who will soon be and is now Beth Eckford, and in his heart, despite the fear and anxiety that had been consuming him, now, upon seeing her, there was only joy and peace.

Love does that.

Thanks be to God.

Amen.

God at Work in You
Ezekiel 18:1-4 and 25-32, and Philippians 2:1-13

One of the great Christian thinkers of history is a Danish philosopher named Soren Kierkegaard. He famously compared the sanctuary and the theater, saying that these two places look the same — both are big rooms with seats in rows turned toward something like a stage. But the difference is this: in the theater the actors are on the stage and you are in the audience, but in here, we are all the actors and it is God who is in the audience.

This description makes sense to me, and I am confident that God, in the audience, loves to hear our choir sing.

That our God rejoices as Cal plays the organ. That God listens as we pray and smiles as children fidget in the pews.

We don't come here to be entertained as we do in a theater, but to direct our attention away from ourselves and towards our Redeemer, for in this hour we are mindful that God draws near. That God is in the audience watching and listening as we worship Him together.

We gather here to offer our praises to God. That's what worship is, and so we try to offer our very best. We don't dress to veg-out on the couch. On Sunday mornings at a church like ours, we dress to bow our heads before our Creator. So, mothers force daughters into dresses, slick down the rebellious hair of 9-year-old boys, and even if they were in the middle of an epic argument for the whole ride over here, families pull it together so they look like a Norman Rockwell painting as they walk in here.

What we do is aspire to some version of perfection.

We rise above the stress and conflict to put on a pretty face.

Even when we know we're not perfect, don't some of us walk into this room pretending to be?

But, in many ways, this is a bad habit.

We humans are in the bad habit of masking despair and conflict, telling everyone around us that everything's fine is when it's not, living a spiritual life of false piety, as though Christianity were one long Stairway to Heaven that we must climb just like the corporate ladder. However, it is in this room that we remember how our God comes near to hear us sing.

We read in our first Scripture Lesson of the God who came near, taking human form:

Let the same mind be in you that was in Christ Jesus,
Who, though he was in the form of God,
Did not regard equality with God as something to be exploited,
But emptied himself,
Taking the form of a slave,
Being born in human likeness.

These are words of the great Christ Hymn that the church in Philippi sang to remember that while we who worship comb our hair, put on our Sunday best, and try to rise to a standard of perfection, God does not call on use to rise to Him for He has come down to us.

That matters, because that changes how we think. That changes how we live.

Knowing that God descended to us changes how we lead.

That's what Paul is writing about here. He writes this letter to address a crisis in leadership. Two leaders in this congregation – Euodia and Syntyche are working against each other, jockeying for control. You've seen this kind of thing before, because conflict is as natural to us humans as sleeping and breathing. Even if we can pull it together to walk into the sanctuary, we are prone to conflict.

A mother used to say that if her children were awake, they were fighting. That's just us, but, if we are Christians, how will we fight? How will we argue?

When God looked down on us and our depravity, He didn't look down in disappointment from the security of Heaven, fire off a few tweets and go back to life as usual. No, God came down from Heaven to see first-hand what was really going on.

That's what parents do – we hear siblings arguing down in the basement – "Don't make me come down there!" we say. So, I've been interested in professional football lately because while protesting during the National Anthem, failing to stand to honor the flag is a complicated and emotional issue. If you watch you'll see that there are those team owners who have remained up in the owner's box, far above the field, and there have been others who descended to the field to lock arms with their players. This is a radical thing to do.

But that's what Paul urges: "Let the same mind be in you that was in Christ Jesus, who though He was in the form of God, did not regard equality with God as something to be exploited."

When God heard the shouting of His children, God could have just brushed some clouds away, looked down, and said, "eh, they'll sort it out eventually."

Or maybe the Son could have said to the Holy Spirit: "What do you think about sending another flood? Wait, we said we wouldn't do that, didn't we?"

No – when God heard our distress, God came down to us, taking the form of a slave, being born in human likeness. And being found in human form, He humbled himself and became obedient to the point of death – even death on a cross.

What then are this bread and this cup? The reminder that God could have stayed up there. Christ could have kept His distance from all our quarreling – but instead, He came right down and offered us His very body and blood.

In His life then is the reminder that love thrives on proximity. That like a mother who holds her baby to her chest, God holds us close. With that example in mind, Paul admonishes us: "Let the same mind be in you that was in Christ Jesus," remembering that when it comes to love, physical distance can be bad.

I once officiated a funeral of a woman whose family rarely visited.

She planned her funeral with me years before she died and chose two Proverbs for the occasion. One was Proverbs 18:24 – "Some friends play at friendship, but a true friend sticks closer than one's nearest kin."

After the service, a friend told me that was an interesting way for her to tell her relatives that they'd be left out of the will. But in this Proverb is a truth that we all know already – we long for closeness and we pity the nursing home resident who no one goes to visit.

Setting the example, what does God do? God shows up, bridges the gap, takes human form. And being found in human form, He humbled himself and became obedient to the point of death – even death on a cross.

This word, "humble" is significant. Just as physical distance can harm relationships, so can arrogance. Failing to be honest with yourself and others can as well. And acting like you're more holy than everybody is just about the worst.

There's a story about John Calvin. His friends said that he was probably the most brilliant man of his generation, but what made it so hard to spend time with him was that he knew it.

In this story about the theologian who founded our tradition is a warning to every Christian so good at pretending that he's perfect, and so are his children, for if Jesus humbled Himself, taking the form of a slave, then what sermon is our life preaching?

The Prophet spoke to the people on the Lord's behalf saying, "The house of Israel says, 'The way of the Lord is unfair.' [But] house of Israel, are my ways unfair? Is it not your ways that are unfair?"

God comes close, but we keep our distance.

God moves into the neighborhood, dwelling among us in Jesus Christ, but we keep our doors locked to our neighbor.

And God humbles Himself, taking the form of a slave, but how many of us take the time to learn the names of the people who clean our homes, our workplaces, or our children's schools?

This is what happens with distance and arrogance – we lose touch with our neighbors because we've lost touch with ourselves.

In order to live the Gospel we must be real.

We must be honest.

We must be human – crying in weakness, listening until we understand, while standing together.

And we must sing, not because we're good at it, but because God likes it.

Ours is a God who has come near – setting the table before us, as though He were the servant - to offer us His very body and blood.

And this God is at work in you. Just as Paul said it of the congregation in Philippi, so it is true here of you.

You – who don't all think the same, who don't all live the same lives, but who worship together.

You who break bread together and join in mission together – delivering meals to neighborhoods that few like to drive through.

You, who have already given up on the illusion of perfection to accept each other as you really are.

The God who comes near to us is at work in you.

Amen.

Not Having a Righteousness of My Own
Isaiah 5:1-7 and Philippians 3:4b-14

A Monday morning can put things in harsh perspective.

Last Monday morning Kelly Dewar's 8-year-old daughter Linley asked her on the way to elementary school drop off (before Kelly had even had her first cup of coffee) about the difference between irony and sarcasm.

Think about that.

This is obviously a question that displays Linley's intelligence, but how did it make Kelly feel? A question like that is a hard way to start your week as a mom.

Instead of starting your week with a feeling that everything is under control and you're fully equipped for the days ahead, a question like that is sure to make you wonder if maybe it might be better to crawl back into bed.

And this is what happened to me. Sara had been quizzing Lily for a quiz on air pollution. "What are three things we can do to fight air pollution Lily?" she asked. Having just dropped the girls off at school on their bikes, I was riding from the school to the church, while proudly thinking about how we're setting the example for our kids here. We're reducing exhaust because we ride our bikes to school. This is great. "In fact," I say to myself, "really, we're setting an example for a whole community. People in their cars are probably thinking – look at that nice family, all fighting air pollution on their daily commute." It was as this self-satisfied thought was passing through my consciousness that I missed a turn, hit a holly bush, and flipped over my handlebars.

It was a good thing someone had suggested that I start wearing a helmet, so the only real damage done was to my ego. As soon as I got up, I scanned the sidewalks to see if there were any witnesses.

There was only one, but that was one too many.

What would Paul say?

Romans 12:3 – "For by the grace given to me I say to everyone among you not to think of yourself more highly than you out to think."

Or to quote our Second Scripture Lesson for this morning: "Yet whatever gains I had, these I have come to regard as loss because of Christ."

What does that mean?

"Yet whatever gains I had, these I have come to regard as loss because of Christ."

In this passage from Philippians, Paul may sound like he's boasting. This morning's second Scripture Lesson begins with his giving us his resume of accomplishments:

-Circumcised on the eighth day

-A member of the people of Israel

-Of the tribe of Benjamin

-A Hebrew born of Hebrews

-As to the law a Pharisee

-As to zeal, a persecutor of the church

-As to righteousness under the law, blameless

But he only lists these accomplishments so that we can see them as he does, in the perspective cast by the next to last. He had done everything that would have rendered him blameless and righteous, but where did that lead him? To persecute Christ's church – to hold the coats as the disciple Stephen was stoned. His intent in sharing his testimony is the same as the intent of that great hymn that we sang just last Sunday:

When I survey the wondrous cross
On which the Prince of glory died,
My richest gain I count but loss,
And pour contempt on all my pride.

You can see the point he's making, and he makes this point hoping that we'll hear it, because like that great church in Philippi to which this letter is addressed, we are like runners who don't do as Paul admonishes us to do: "forgetting what lies behind and straining forward to what lies ahead;" for even while we run this race in faith, we are busy looking back to see whom we're ahead of.

We're like a certain self-satisfied bike rider, busy judging the minivans that pass by for contributing to air pollution and not realizing that there's a holly bush up ahead.

There's a sense in which competition can be good. We all know that. We want to win, but think of the lady in the restaurant moving her arm back and forth, trying to trick her fit bit into thinking that she really did get all her steps in.

Think of the athlete so set on winning that he sacrifices his body to drugs.

Consider the football player who sees himself not as a boy in high school, but as a god among boys, walking the hall with an air of self-importance because he can throw a football further than anyone else.

Is he not also a vineyard of wild grapes?

That image of the wild grapes growing in the tended vineyard comes both from our Call to Worship (based on Psalm 80) and on Isaiah's point in the 5th chapter that we read as our First Scripture Lesson. The claim is that while we were created by God, redeemed from slavery in Egypt and from slavery to sin, we were planted in this fertile valley by a God who removed the stones and tilled the land. Despite all this preparation, all these blessings, rather than yield a bountiful harvest, we are a vineyard of wild grapes.

But we think of ourselves as Chardonnay.

A man named Roy Brown told me a story once. He played on the Presbyterian College tennis team after serving in World War II. After graduation he always sent in a contribution through the alumni association to the tennis program at Presbyterian College. In his 80's he received a special invitation to the ribbon cutting of the new tennis courts, and as we sometimes do, he began wondering why he received this invitation to this event. "What if they've named the courts after me?" he imagined.

I would have encouraged him to think this way. After all, he was a veteran, a member of the tennis team, and a long-time contributor, but when they called him down on the court during the ceremony it was to present him with a coffee mug.

'Most expensive coffee mug I've ever had," he told me.

Why is it that rather than run this race in faith, we want to be first in line?

Why is it that rather than confess our struggles to our neighbors, we're more interested in bragging to them about our European vacations?

Why is it that while we are all in this life together, all imperfect people just doing the best that we can:

— that while not even one of us has enough righteousness to save herself from sin

— that while we are all sinners, redeemed, not by our own work, but only by the grace of God

We all still love to imagine that we are winning all on our own while looking back and to see who's doing worse?

Back in Tennessee, the United Methodist Church across the street had this pastor who would fall asleep during the choir anthem. Everybody was talking about him and I was enjoying it, egging this on really, until Sara says, "You be careful Joe, because you know how this will hurt when it's you they're talking about."

Sara was right.

She nearly always is.

There's a log in this eye, and for too long preachers and Christians alike have been walking around, one-upping each other, when really, if Paul says that he has no righteousness of his own I don't know who we think we are.

No matter how much time I spend in prayer.

No matter how much more mature I am now than when I was in High School.

No matter how low my emissions, thanks to my bicycle, I'm still just a vineyard of wild grapes who by the grace of God has been given the honor of running this race with you.

That's the difference between a Monday and a Sunday morning.

On a Monday we feel like we are supposed to have it all together, but on a Sunday we don't have to pretend. We don't have to look back. Because again, we've all done it together — publicly prayed it out loud in our Prayer of Confession:

You taught us peace, but we wage war.
You forgive us, while we withhold forgiveness from our neighbor.
You seek us out, while we hide our face from you. Forgive us Lord

– for when you expected grapes, we yielded wild grapes – but by the Grace of God – there is something wonderful happening in here.

When I think of this church and all that we've been through in the past few years I think of that Psalm that made up our Call to Worship:

We are a vine, brought out of Egypt.
Planted in fertile soil.
God cleared the ground, and the mountains were covered by our shade.

You remember it then as I do. Years ago, there were so many of us that when we sent the youth group to the Montreat Youth Conference they nearly took the whole thing over. We were one of the largest Presbyterian Churches in the South.

But then our walls were broken down, so that those who passed along could just pluck our fruit. In those days I was up in Tennessee wondering why as I know all of you were.

I don't know exactly why God would permit such a thing to happen.

Some have called it pruning, and I like that.

But regardless, I know that God has heard our cry.

I know that our God looked down from heaven to see, and has renewed His regard for this vine, and now I can't walk in our doors without feeling that the Holy Spirit fills this place. But here's what we all must remember - that's why the Holy Spirit fills this place.

That's why there is joy and laughter within these walls.

It's not me, and I know that. Listen – I'm still just the kid who skipped out of Sunday School to run the halls and steal cookies out of the preschool cupboards. Like Paul and like you, it's not that "I have already obtained [anything] or have already reached the goal; but I press on to make it my own, because Christ Jesus has made me his own."

That's what we must always be about.

Sometimes we are so desperate to see something good in ourselves that we only look for bad in our neighbor; and sometimes we are so practiced in celebrating ourselves that we take credit for what only God can do.

And what has God done – revived us again. Let us forget "what lies behind, staring forward to what lies ahead – the goal for the prize of the heavenly call of God in Christ Jesus."

Amen.

Part 3

Stewardship

There's nothing easy about asking the members of your church for money, but each Stewardship Season when I preach sermons encouraging the congregation to fill out a pledge card, I reflect on the importance of using the gifts we've all been given of time, talent, and treasure to the Glory of God.

My most vivid memory of what stewardship really means is embodied in a young man named Mike who tithed to his small country church his pig. For some reason Mike's pastor thought I might know what to do with a pig, and he called and asked for my help while we were both serving churches in Tennessee. Now a painting of a pig hangs on my office wall reminding me of what Mike gave his church and what I might offer the Lord.

I was once again inspired by Mike when I wrote the following sermons that made up a series on Stewardship.

Your Faith in God has Become Known
Isaiah 45:1-7 and 1 Thessalonians 1:1-10

I've just read the opening to a letter. That's what 1 Thessalonians is, a letter, and letters are interesting things. I remember running out to the mailbox after elementary school, going through all the letters only to be disappointed because everything was addressed to my Dad. I didn't know anything about bills back then, so only now do I see the benefit of mail that's addressed to someone else; however, I wish this letter that I've just read were addressed to us.

In a sense, it is.

We believe that Paul wrote this letter that we call 1 Thessalonians to a church in Greece, in the city of Thessalonica, and like we often do when the letter is particularly meaningful, this church saved his letter. We know they did because we have it now and can read it as they once did.

I think it would have been an honor to receive this letter, because Paul's words here in the first chapter are so encouraging.

It would have been extremely encouraging to read: "We always give thanks to God for all of you and mention you in our prayers." And it would have been a matter of great pride to read: "In every place your faith in God has become known, so that we have no need to speak about it."

Think about that.

Paul wrote these words to the church in Thessalonica because the neighboring Christian communities would brag on them to Paul. We read there in verse 9: "The people of those regions report about us what kind of welcome we had among you, and how you turned to God from idols, to serve a living, and true God."

Two things then – offering hospitality and turning away from idolatry.

We can do that.

But that requires knowing what idolatry is.

What is idolatry?

On the one hand, it's obvious. It's number one on the 10 Commandments, a copy of which is displayed right by our front doors that once hung in the Cobb County Court House: "You shalt have no other gods before me," it reads.

What's idolatry then? It's worshiping something else, somebody else, giving anything the kind of priority in your life that only God should have.

A good example of idolatry from the Old Testament is the Golden Calf from the book of Exodus. You know the story well. Moses went up on a mountain to get the 10 Commandments and when he came back down, these people who had been without his supervision while he was up on Mount Horeb, had melted down their gold to make a calf that they worshiped.

They shouldn't have done that. That's idolatry. And on the one hand we don't do that now. Paul might as well be proud of us just as he was of those members of the Thessalonian Church who had turned to God from idols, to serve a living and true God.

We don't have any Golden Calves around. The closest thing to a golden calf around here that I could think of is that statue of Alexander Stephens Clay on Glover Square, which doesn't count because a statue isn't the same thing as an idol. We don't worship Alexander Stephens Clay, but this statue which I take a moment to look at every time I walk through the Square so I can check on this hornets' nest sheltered right under the front of his overcoat does help to describe what idolatry is, because while I was checking on the hornets last Wednesday I finally read the inscription at the base of the statue. It reads: "Alexander Stephens Clay – his life was largely given to the service of his people."

Idolatry. What is idolatry? One form of idolatry is selfishness, because the devotion that should only be given to God is given instead to self. Alexander Stephens Clay lived a life "largely given to the service of people," but too many of us live a life consumed with ourselves.

Selfishness then is a form of idolatry.

The great preacher and theologian Fredrick Buechner describes idolatry as the practice of ascribing absolute value to things of relative worth, and in saying that selfishness is a form of idolatry I don't mean that the self is worthless, but that plenty of people go around trying to make themselves happy by thinking only of themselves. When that's the case what happens is they make themselves miserable.

I have this friend whose father spent all of his money on this beautiful house in Montana. The scenery is magnificent, but his wife divorced him, his children never come to visit, so this friend of mine told me that his father's home is basically a prison cell with the most beautiful view you've ever seen.

Idolatry. Selfish idolatry will leave you empty and alone.

So, when Paul applauds the church at Thessalonica for turning away from idolatry, what we must see is that they turned from death to life ...

From giving devotion to the created to giving devotion to the Creator.

They turned away from chasing after all that will never lead to true fulfillment and towards the only thing that ever will.

What they did was they turned away from idolatry, and we must do the same because we worship idols as well. I know that to be true, not because we have graven images all over our houses that we need to get rid of, but because if you looked at our credit card statements you'd be able to tell what it is that we think is going to lead to abundant life.

We live in a culture of idolatry I believe.

We worship fun and entertainment.

We spend our money on toys that we think will make us happy, but you know what they say, "The two happiest days for a boat owner are the day that he bought it and the day that he sold it."

Why would we spend our money on what won't make us happy?

Why would we go into debt for things that won't make us happy?

I don't know, but I'm good at doing it.

Before I checked on the hornets' nest, I spent $20.00 on a salad. And I was hungry again about 15 minutes later.

What will fill us up?

What will lead to fulfillment, satisfaction, and joy?

It's there on the statue: "A life largely given to the service of his people."

A life largely given to the service of his God.

To some degree I learned that a long time ago.

My parents taught Sunday School here. They modeled for my brother, sister, and me what it means to give yourself to something larger than yourself, so it seemed only natural to go with the youth group on the Mexico Mission Trip following my freshman year of High School.

I remember being intimidated by the days of travel in an old bus that was reported to have air conditioning but mostly didn't. My shirt would stick to the red vinyl seats. We'd spend the night in cheap hotels. And then when we finally made it to the border we'd get stuck for hours because Rev. Robert Hay refused to bribe the customs officials.

All this we'd go through, and why? Because there were families down there who needed houses, and back home I would have spent that week sleeping late and watching TV. Down there we were stacking cinderblocks and mixing cement, and nothing could have made me happier.

Selfishness is idolatry, you see, because the cult of selfishness tells you to treat yourself, to buy your way to happiness. But devotion to such an idol will only lead to the same emptiness you felt before – only this time you'll be surrounded by a bunch of stuff you don't need.

You want to talk about joy.

You want to talk about abundant life.

Then you must talk about living your life for a higher purpose, turning away from the cult of self-centered idolatry that permeates everything in our culture, from the merchandise at Target to the storage unit where that merchandise will eventually be stored. We must turn from idolatry so that we can live the kind of abundant life that Jesus talked about, of loving your neighbor as yourself ...

Of living a life largely given to the service of our people.

Of being a part of the good that our God is doing in the world.

And when we turn away from all the false gods of our 21st century culture – the gods of war who promise peace but only give more violence – the gods of greed that keep our eyes searching for pleasure around every corner while keeping satisfaction ever out of reach – the gods of self-interest, self-love, and self-consumption who worship at the temple of narcissism and whose priests deliver their message on your televisions, phones, and computers by calling you to fame and fortune – when we turn to God from these idols, to serve a living and true God, then we are a part of the great act of salvation that our Creator is enacting in our world.

We read there in Isaiah:

I am the Lord, and there is no one besides me;
I am the Lord, and there is no other.
I form light and create darkness,
I make weal and create woe;
I the Lord do all these things – and is his presence not among us now?

Like the vibrations of the train, does God's presence not resonate through these walls?

Resound from our rooftop?

So why would we worship in the temple of self-interest, bowing before the American Idols, chasing after the dreams of the soulless, when we have been invited to proclaim the Gospel of the Living God?

Stewardship Season begins today, and as a guiding phrase, this year's committee adopted 2 Corinthians 9:8, "Share abundantly in every good work."

It's not just that we want you to share what you have (and we do want you to share what you have), it's that we want you to share in the work that the God of Creation is doing here in this place.

We have been invited to participate in the redeeming work of our lord Jesus Christ.

We have been invited to serve the living and true God.

We have been invited to give our time, our treasure, our pigs, and our hearts so that the Kingdom would be advanced and so our joy would be complete.

Yesterday at a Presbytery Meeting they took up an offering. I didn't have any cash, and I was embarrassed. Martie Moore could tell, so she gave me a dollar. Denise Lobodinski did the same. It felt good to put money in the plate.

Mike Velardi told me that a chicken brought a basket of eggs to the farmhouse, proud of her contribution, until she saw the pig, which stood before the smokehouse prepared to make a real commitment. While we want real commitments this year, let me say this – Stewardship isn't about giving until it hurts. Stewardship is about giving until it feels so good you can't imagine not doing it.

Share abundantly in every good work.

Share abundantly in all the good work that we are already doing.

Share abundantly in all the good that we will be doing with your help.

Amen.

The Great Ordeal Will Not Stop Them[2]
1 John 3:1-3 and Revelation 7:9-17

Revelation is really something.

There's a part of me that always wants to avoid it. It's a book of the Bible that's hard to understand, but plenty of people think they know what it means, and so many people who don't know have tried to tell us, and now we all carry baggage to this book of the Bible with all its symbols and prophecy.

But we can't just avoid Revelation because it's a wonderful book of the Bible, an important book of the Bible, and if we let fear of this book get the best of us, then we'll miss out on all the beauty that it contains.

The passage that I've just read is full of beauty. There's this great multitude – so big that no one could count – from every nation, from all tribes and peoples and languages. They're all there in Heaven and they're singing, "Salvation belongs to our God."

This is a powerful image.

And just the composition of this group is enough of a subject to preach a sermon. There is this great big diverse group in heaven and one of the elders addresses the author of the book, who's also the narrator, the visionary. This one elder asks John, "Who are these, robed in white, and where have they come from?"

The elder wants to know who is this great big diverse group that just arrived in Heaven, and the meaning of his question is like that old joke Presbyterians tell about Baptists. One Presbyterian arrives in Heaven and says to another Presbyterian, "Why all the whispering up here?" And the other Presbyterian says, "Because God put the Baptists just on the other side of that hill and they think they're the only ones who made it here. We don't want to spoil it for them."

There are all kinds of people in this world, aren't there? And some people believe that they're the only ones with the answers, that they're the only ones who have a right to the Kingdom. But in our world, there are all kinds of people who believe different things and who come from different places. Every color,

---

2 Tom Tate, *Feasting on the Word, Year A, Volume 4* (Louisville: Westminster John Knox, 2011) 222.

shape, and size, they are precious in his eyes, Jesus loves the little children of the world.[3]

We've been singing some version of that song for a long time, but the words are still radical.

An old friend back in Tennessee told me one time that it's not just that the members of West 7th Street Church of Christ think that Presbyterians are going to Hell, it's that the members of West 7th Street Church of Christ think that the folks over at Graymere Church of Christ are going to Hell, and so are the members of Mt. Calvary Church of Christ. They think they're the only ones going, just like this Elder who asks, "Who are these, robed in white?"

So, according to Scripture, who are these, robed in white?

They're the children of God. That's who they are. And I'm one. So are you ... just as are the little children who come to Club 3:30 for after-school care and tutoring ... as are our neighbors in this great big diverse county in which we find ourselves.

There are all kinds of people in God's Kingdom, and that's good.

I met a different kind of a person last Wednesday morning. I was standing on the corner at the cross walk waiting for the cars to stop so I could walk. But you know this kind of lady. She wasn't waiting for anyone, and she just walked right into that crosswalk with authority and the traffic stopped for her.

Or it almost did. One car scooted in front of her and she yelled at the driver, "I'm walking here!" I said, "Lady, I like your style," and she showed me this whistle she has around her neck that she uses to blow at the cars that don't respect the cross walk. I laughed, and she told me that her husband said he's going to buy her a paintball gun so she can mark the cars that don't stop for pedestrians.

I was amazed by this lady. And only later did I put it together that here was this lady, standing up to oncoming traffic, the day after a man in a rented truck from Home Depot killed eight people driving down a bike path in Manhattan.

And what's worse – he did it in the name of religion.

---

[3] https://shanebertou.wordpress.com/2007/07/24/wait-red-and-yellow-those-darn-racist-bible-songs/

Now he claims to be a fundamentalist Muslim, and some people get caught up in that. But I want to say that this crazy idea of one person having all the answers and everyone else being so wrong that they're less than human is an idea that can infect every religion and every person. Any Christian who falls for this idea that religion is about your being right and everyone else being wrong has never met the Jesus that I know.

There's this whole multitude up there. One elder is wondering who they are because that's a weird human defect we suffer from – the idea that "I have it right and everyone else must have it wrong". The idea that I matter more! That my agenda is so important that these other people in my way aren't people but speed bumps!

The extreme version, the sick version, is what we saw last Tuesday in Manhattan. But there's a problem when any and all of us are so busy rushing through life with an overblown sense of our own importance that we fail to stop and consider the people in the crosswalk.

Hurrying as though eternity depended on what happens in the next 15 minutes.

We can't speed through life.

And, we can't get so caught up in our daily routine that we are fooled into thinking that our lives constantly hang in the balance.

I'm prone to that kind of anxiety, but not everybody is. Our Associate Pastor, Rev. Joe Brice seems immune to it.

I was rushing around doing something one day and I realized I had forgotten to give Joe some piece of important information. Worried that he'd be as anxious about it as I was, I apologized to him and Joe responded, "Man, that's no big deal. Don't worry about me. Everything that really matters to me has already happened."

"Everything that really matters to me has already happened," says the sage of Paulding County.

And like Joe Brice, these saints in the book of Revelation are defined by what has already happened.

You see, they are those who have come out of the great ordeal. And we don't know exactly what that is, but from the book of Revelation we can infer that the great ordeal is a time of suffering and religious persecution ... a time in human history when life is challenging ... when money is in short supply ...

when life is lived under the shadow of an oppressive government ... when war is the rule and not the exception ... and when hardship surrounds us, and every day seems a grueling struggle to make it from one day to the next.

What makes this multitude dressed in white exceptional is that these saints have come out of the great ordeal, but the great ordeal has not stopped them from singing.

They can see what God has done.

They know the gift that God has given.

And no matter the hardship and pain, it can't overshadow the redemption and the joy.

No matter the oppression, it can't touch the freedom that they have in Christ.

No matter the struggle, they say, how can I keep from singing?

For my life goes on in endless song
Above earth's lamentation.
I hear the real, though far off hymn
That hails the new creation.
Above the tumult and the strife,
I heard the music ringing;
It sounds an echo in my soul
How can I keep from singing?

That's what they sing. Because everything that really matters has already happened. For Christ has died, Christ has risen, and Christ will come again.

That's why tyrants tremble, sick with fear.

They hear their death-knell ringing,
And friends rejoice both far and near,
So how can I keep from singing.

Life can seem like a struggle, but the struggle cannot be what defines us because what defines us, we whose robes have been washed in the blood of the Lamb, is the great act of Christ's salvation.

Our lives then, which have already been saved from the pit, must not be a hurried mess or a stress-filled struggle, but a great song lifted to the One who created us, redeemed us, and sustains us still.

Our First Scripture Lesson from 1 John said it all: "See what love the Father has given us, that we should be called children of God," and that is what we are. So, live your life, not complacent in the struggle, but singing your part with the great choir of angels and all the saints in light, giving your time, your talent, your treasure, to the glory of God the Father. Do as so many saints of this church whom we will remember later in the service have already done. Those saints who were such stewards of their lives that they made this church what it is today.

A pledge card was given to you this morning with your bulletin, and it's important to consider what it is and what it means. I pray that it will cause you to stop, to take a break from the fever of life so that you can reflect on the gifts that you have received, and to take the time to show your thanks to the One who always gives us a reason to sing. For the Great Ordeal of Life must not stop us either.

Amen.

They Were Stewards of their Lives
Micah 3:5-12 and Matthew 23:1-12

I heard a joke at a Kiwanis meeting last week. Andrew Macintosh and I were proud to be the guests of Margaret Waldrep, and after lunch the speaker was introduced. Buck Rogers is his name. He's the president of the State Bar of Georgia, and he gets up there and he asks the group, "Do you know how many lawyers there are in the state of Georgia?" And some smart aleck in the back shouts out: "Too many."

I like lawyer jokes, and I like them a lot better than preacher jokes.

A group of kids were standing around having a lying contest, and the preacher overheard them. Offended by the idea that they'd compete in telling the biggest lie rather than practice being trustworthy and honest, he marches over there and tells them, "You boys should stop telling those lies and should be more like me. I always tell the truth."

They look at each other, and then shout: "You win pastor! That's the biggest lie we ever heard."

This morning Scripture demands that we come face to face with the reality that the Church is not nearly so unlike Wall Street or Washington as I would like. That those many politicians, so self-serving as to be completely ineffective, that those business executives, so cutthroat as to worship the mighty dollar, are not so unlike a lot of clergy I know.

I went through college and seminary preparing myself to be different. I thought that I would be real, faithful, and honest, but every day I face the same reality of being human and appearing far more like a Pharisee than I would like.

Jesus's warning to them could be directed at me just as well.

Jesus said that they do all their deeds to be seen by others. And last Wednesday Night, there I was, finally in the kitchen, cooking for Wednesday Night Supper, so proud of myself that I put my picture all over Facebook, because I love to have all my deeds seen by others too.

Did you see me posing with that pot? Jesus said that the Pharisees do all their deeds to be seen by others, and I must be careful about that.

Jesus also said that, "They love to have the place of honor at banquets and the best seats in the synagogues" and have you seen where I get to sit in here? Right up front.

Then those Pharisees – Jesus said that they love to be greeted with respect in the marketplaces, to have people call them Rabbi. Maybe we don't have a marketplace and maybe no one calls me Rabbi, but watch me walk through Kroger, scanning the aisle for whom I might know. Unless I'm in the beer aisle, that is.

I am a sinner. There's no doubt about it, but this is a reality that I can't run away or hide from. Instead, this is a reality that I must come to terms with. Because, here I am up in this pulpit! I have on this fancy robe and this microphone that makes me feel like Madonna. But every time I put the stole around my neck, do you know what I think of?

This stole represents the towel that Jesus used to wash the disciples' feet.

We preachers need to remember that, because the model of Jesus is a different model than the world of business or commerce, politics or power.

I'm not the CEO of First Presbyterian Church of Marietta, Georgia. No – to quote the Psalms: I'm a **doorkeeper** in the house of my God.

That's what I am. A sinner who can write a sermon and lead you in prayer, invited to help keep the doors of this mighty house of God open. Don't let me forget that, because bringing honor to myself, falling down that trap that the Pharisees fell into, will lead to the kind of self-serving misery that I long to avoid, for there is no more miserable person than the one who seeks only to honor himself.

There's a better way to live, and Jesus shows us how.

Think about him – the Creator of the Universe, who comes down from Heaven to wash the disciples' feet.

The all-powerful God – who takes on human sin and dies a criminal's death.

We know that He is full of mercy and truth. That He is all divinity and majesty, but He lived a human's life to proclaim a mighty Gospel.

Live this way, He says. Not like those Pharisees who teach one thing and then do another – no – remember that the greatest among you will be your servant.

All who exalt themselves will be humbled, and all who humble themselves will be exalted.

Think about that. And remember: there's no more miserable person than the one who always tries to get ahead without thinking of her neighbors.

Joanne and Jim Taylor are different.

You might know Joanne and Jim. They don't live far from here – just over the railroad tracks and off Maple Street. Joanne and Jim Taylor were sitting on their porch one evening, talking about the lot across from their house, thinking that if the lot ever came up for sale, how they'd like to buy it. Well, two weeks later it did come up for sale. Jim was out of town, so Joanne called him and told him that she was ready to make an offer.

Jim asked her what she'd like to do with the property. She didn't want to fix up the little house that was on it; she'd rather just tear the house down, plant some flowers and turn it into a little park for the neighbors. That's what she told her husband.

Jim thought that sounded fine, as long as she didn't put any tacky yard art out in it. Well, you might know, especially if you live somewhere along Maple, that Jim relented on the tacky yard art. In fact, the 6-foot cowboy boot that sits out there is his doing, and he just ordered his wife Joanne a life size cow statue to put out there for Christmas.

These two bought a park, and I wanted to understand why they did it, so as Martie Moore and I were talking to Joanne last Tuesday (Martie and I like to patrol the neighborhood every once in a while) you could just tell that she loved her park. She didn't even mind it when other people used it. In fact, she was on vacation and her neighbors called to tell her that someone was having a wedding out there and asked if she knew anything about it.

She didn't, and she didn't mind at all, because the park doesn't make her any money. It doesn't do anything that she can put her finger on; it just makes her happy.

That's a big deal, and she's not the only one.

Harold is like that.

A lady named Dawn Taylor told me his story.

She wrote about it and it appeared in the local paper back in our town in Tennessee. She's the lady in charge of the Family Center, an organization there that's a lot like our MUST Ministries. People who need something to eat go there, homeless people who need a shower go there, and every year there's a big drive to raise money for Thanksgiving turkeys so that every family in Columbia, Tennessee has a big, happy Thanksgiving.

Well, Harold heard about it.

Harold sleeps in his car and every month he receives a disability check, so he has money to eat but he sleeps in his car and he uses the shower at the Family Center. Last week he walked right into Dawn Taylor's office and gave her $23.00.

"I saw you were collecting turkeys in the newspaper. I want to help, I want to buy someone a turkey." That's what he said.

Dawn wouldn't take the money. She said, "Harold, you're homeless. You can't give me any money. You need that money." But he insisted, saying, "I saw the article in the paper. I want to help. It's not Thanksgiving unless you are eating turkey and watching the ball game. I want to help someone do that."

Can you imagine?

Where's he going to watch the ballgame?

Where's he going to cook his turkey?

Why is he giving away his last $23.00?

Because it is better to give than to receive.

Because there is something there in our hearts - we've been preprogramed to think of the needs of others.

We stop being whom God created us to be when we become self-consumed like the Pharisees, and so Jesus taught us to love our neighbors as ourselves.

And Harold wasn't giving until it hurt.

No, he gave and as a result there's this joy that just oozes out of him. Don't you want some of that?

You can have it.

I know that so many of you already do. Because you gave it to me.

One of the most wonderful things that's happened since coming here is introducing my two daughters to my third grade Sunday School teacher.

Mrs. Florrie Corley – for years she did that.

And then there was Tim Hammond who drove me back and forth to Mexico beginning when I was around 14 years old. This was back when he was about 10 feet tall. He's still doing it, and there are plenty of people who would like to know why.

Why would Jimmy Scarr show up here every Sunday night to feed our youth group?

Or these days - what is Mike Velardi doing with an apron around his neck every Wednesday by 1:00 in our church kitchen and why does he stay from then until the last pot is clean?

Why does Melissa Ricketts work 60 hours every week and then sit up there with the cameras for two services every Sunday morning?

Why?

Why? Because it feels good – that's why.

Our Stewardship theme this year came from 2 Corinthians: "Share abundantly in every blessing," and I want you to know that I'm not talking about sharing abundantly in every burden, sharing abundantly in every bill, or sharing abundantly in every grueling task that it takes to keep this church going. I'm talking about inviting you to share in the blessing of living out your life for a bigger purpose.

Thinking of others beside yourself.

Knowing the true joy that giving brings.

And finding out that when you do – God takes what you offer and does far more than you could ever imagine.

Think about Mike's pig.

Think about how God used Mike's pig.

You see – some would say, "But I'm just a regular guy." Or "I'm just a little old lady." Or "Who am I to be used by God for some great big purpose?" But that's the strength of our Scripture Lesson for today. We clergy are tempted to think that we know everything and that God can use only us. But again and again, experience teaches me that the Church is the sign of God doing miraculous things through us.

I remember the first Sunday our daughter Lily got to sit in big church with her friend, McKennon Jones. They were 3 or 4 years old, and when I walked into the sanctuary and got up to the pulpit, McKennon looks to Lily and asks, "What's Joe doing up there?"

And Lily says, "I don't know."

A long time ago I knew that I wanted to give my life to ministry. When I meet my Maker I want to hear that sure I binge watched the second Season of *Stranger Things* on TV, but for the most part I used my life to do some good.

How much more will that be said of each veteran who stood this morning, they who have given their lives for a higher purpose.

Have not they been good stewards of their lives, setting an example for us to follow?

They were stewards of our lives, and their example calls us to "go and do likewise." Just as the needs of our Church today and our world out there call us to action. But if you investigate your heart, you'll know that you need it too.

Take your pledge card – consider your gift – and use your life, your treasure, your time to make this church stronger – to make the witness of this church louder so that our world in need will hear some good news.

Be a good steward of your life and "Share Abundantly in Every Blessing."

Amen.

Part 4

From Christ the King to Christmas

Too often our post-Thanksgiving focus is on physical gifts that we might give, rather than the great gift that God has given. The following sermons, preached from Christ the King Sunday through the season of Advent and on into Christmas, are from my first Christmas serving First Presbyterian Church of Marietta, Georgia. During this first Advent I was inspired by the following quote from Dr. Walter Brueggemann:

Advent issues a vision of another day, written by the poet, given to Israel midst the deathly cadence. We do not know when, but we know for sure. The poet knows for sure that this dying and killing is not forever, because another word has been spoken [but will we hear it?][4]

4 Walter Brueggemann, *Devotions for Advent: Celebrating Abundance* (Westminster John Knox Press, Louisville, 2017) 10.

All We Like Sheep
Ezekiel 34:11-16 and 20-24, and Matthew 25:31-46

The book of Genesis begins our Bible and tells us that out of an outpouring of love, God created the heavens, the earth, and the living things which inhabit the earth. On the earth, the Creator set a garden, and in this garden, among other things, there was notably a man, a woman, a serpent, and a forbidden tree.

You know the story. You know that the Creator said to the man, "You may freely eat of every tree of the garden, but of the tree of the knowledge of good and evil you shall not eat." This was clear enough instruction, drawing the line between obedience and disobedience. But of course the serpent suggested to the woman that they eat from it, and she did. Then she took some to her husband who was with her, and he ate.

This was wrong, but it gets worse. After they ate, they heard the Lord God walking in the garden at the time of the evening breeze, and the man and his wife hid themselves from the presence of the Lord God among the trees of the garden.

The Lord God called to the man, and asked him, "Where are you?"

They were hiding, because that's what people who have been disobedient do.

Years ago, we were 10 or 11 years old and had the great idea that we'd explore the great big storm drain running beneath the Charlton Forge neighborhood where we lived. I don't remember that we were explicitly forbidden from doing so. Maybe our parents never imagined that we'd do such a thing, but we didn't want to risk missing out, so, without permission, we explored the underbelly of our neighborhood, and when I went back home my parents asked me what I had been doing.

Assuming that they didn't want me exploring the sewer, I told them I had just been over at Matt Buchanan's house, which was sort of the truth, though it didn't explain why I smelled so bad. When the truth came out I was grounded for two weeks, not only because I had been in the sewer, but because I lied about it too.

Such a two-fold ethical failure is what Church history calls the "Fall of Man." Since the beginning, since the second chapter of Genesis, we have been falling and falling again – first with an act of disobedience, then the cover-up which always makes things worse. This is the human condition. All we like sheep have gone astray.

That chorus was in my mind this week as I read two of the many passages of Scripture that describe God's people as sheep. This morning we have two Scripture passages where humans are personified as sheep, and so the song that was in my mind while reading this last week was that great chorus from Handel's *Messiah*: "All we like sheep, have gone astray."

That's true.

And what's worse is that once we've gone astray, we lie like Joe Evans or we hide like Adam and Eve. Why would we hide?

We hide because we misunderstand love. We assume that the natural result of going astray must be rejection, but that's not so with a loving God.

Here's another familiar Bible story — a young man asks for his inheritance before his father has even died. He takes the money and squanders it on loose living. Loose living is exactly what you imagine it is — all the money's gone, spent on things that nice people don't spend money on. Having squandered it, he's afraid to return home. Instead, he works as a laborer for so little that he winds up jealous of the pigs, who at least have pods to eat in their slop bucket.

Only in desperation does he return home. Realizing that his father's hired hands live better than this and hoping to become one of them, he goes back. But upon his return, his father rushes out to embrace him and treats him like a long-lost prince.

Why? Because this is who God is. This is whom the Bible describes God to be — not just the one who created us and legislated the great commands to guide our behavior, for the God of Scripture is also the Father who so deeply longs for His son to return home that He is full of forgiveness. The God of Scripture is a Husband who's love for His wife can never die — the God of Scripture is a Shepherd who goes after the lost sheep even through they've gone astray, trapped in the brambles of fallenness.

All we like sheep have gone astray, and the great God of heaven and earth longs to gather us in — For thus says the Lord God (from the book of Ezekiel): "I myself will search for my sheep and will seek them out. As shepherds seek out their flocks when they are among their scattered sheep, so I will seek out my sheep."

That's God. That's Scripture.

Can you believe that?

I hope you can – because it's hard for me sometimes. Sometimes I go back to that image of God that I remember from fiery, manipulative preachers who convinced me that the question was not whether I'd be going to Hell, just how soon.

However, the message of Christianity as recorded in Scripture is not condemnation for the imperfect. The Bible is not a record of continued abuse on the fallen. No, in the pages of Scripture are the magnificent stories of grace for the lost, and so that great hymn goes like this:

Amazing Grace, how sweet the sound
That saved a wretch like me
I once was lost but now am found
Was blind but now I see

All we like sheep have gone astray, and the Shepherd longs to bring us home. That's Christianity. Not perfection, not condemnation, not self-righteousness, not judgmental legalism that calls some good and some bad – no. Instead, this faith of ours is all about the Great Good News that Jesus Christ, Lord of all, created you and redeemed you, and now wants you to come home. If you're too ashamed, the Good Shepherd will even go out to find you so that he can bring you back.

Here's again what we read from the book of Ezekiel: "I myself will be the shepherd of my sheep…I will seek the lost, and I will bring back the strayed, and I will bind up the injured, and I will strengthen the weak."

But there's a catch.

The catch is in the next verse from our First Scripture Lesson: "But the fat and the strong I will destroy. I will feed them with justice."

And our Second Scripture Lesson put it another way.

In this last parable of the 25th chapter of the Gospel of Matthew, the final separation of the sheep and the goats, we hear that there will be no entry into the Kingdom of Heaven without a recommendation from the poor, the imprisoned, the sick, the least of these. If you believe that all we like sheep have gone astray but are welcomed home, if you've accepted that kind of grace and that kind of undeserved salvation remembering that once you were lost – once you were blind – that once you were wretched – then ask yourself, "How can I not offer my kindred lost sheep the same grace that I have received?

If you believe that all we like sheep have gone astray but are welcomed home, then you must be ready to pass grace on to other people who don't deserve it either.

And that's hard – because once you've made it, it's easy to forget where you came from.

If all we like sheep have gone astray, then we all must remember who we were.

Life as a redeemed sheep must be different. We must avoid self-righteousness.

The ones who won't even speak the word divorce.

The ones who pretend like their houses are always clean.

That relative who makes you feel insecure when she asks about your children because you know what she's really listening for. You know this lady – you probably saw her at Thanksgiving. Human nature sometimes slips in a moment of weakness, and there are those who call themselves Christians but who rejoice in pointing out the speck in their neighbor's eye, blind to the log in their own, having long forgotten that all we like sheep may go astray.

But we, who have received grace, cannot disassociate from those who need it.

We cannot operate according to the rules of middle school or proper society.

Because while many of us are mindful of being seen with the right kind of people, with whom we are seen matters to Jesus too, and he expects you and me to be seen with the lost.

His law is so different from the law of middle school, for according to Scripture, the hand extended with dirt under the nails and no shoes on his feet is He who holds the Keys to the Kingdom.

The voice that's dry and raspy, lips cracked – "Sir, if only I had some water to drink" – it is this One who shows us the way to Eternal Life.

The stranger who walks into town with a name that no one recognizes from a place that no one has ever heard of – she has an invitation for you and me. For she invites us to return grace to the one we received it from.

For some who sought salvation asked: "Lord, when was it that we saw you hungry and gave you food, or thirsty and gave you something to drink? And when was it that we saw you a stranger and welcomed you, or naked and gave you clothing? And when was it that we saw you sick or in prison and visited you?"

These are questions that the condemned ask, because they failed to offer their kindred lost sheep the same grace that they once received.

May these words guide your behavior: "Truly I tell you, just as you did it to one of the least of these who are members of my family, you did it to me."

All we like sheep have gone astray, and we can't forget it. Because we, the lost sheep who have been found, are obligated to share the same grace that we once received.

Amen.

Restore us, O God; Let Your Face Shine, That We May Be Saved
Psalm 80:1-7 and 17-19, and Isaiah 64:1-9

Today is a special day. All Sundays are special, of course. I used to work with a Music Director who said that the most important Sunday of the year is the next one coming up. But today is a special Sunday, the first Sunday of Advent, plus we have these new hymnals, and we have Communion.

I have an early memory of Communion here at this church.

I was a couple years older than Doug and Andy Miller, twins, and close friends with Mikey Buchanan, and the first time those three could sit by themselves in a worship service was a communion Sunday.

I guess they were 8 or 9 years old, and when the bread came, they did just what they were supposed to do, but when the cup came, before drinking, they all toasted each other with the tiny little communion cups.

It's amazing what kids do without their parents sitting close by, but the truth of the matter is that when no one is watching, all people act a little differently. Even a little bit of freedom can be dangerous for anyone.

I remember the first-time wine was served at Sara's family's Thanksgiving dinner. It was several years ago now, and when we gathered around the Thanksgiving table with my wife Sara's family, the adult places at the table came complete with a wine glass, and while that may sound normal enough, this is something that never would have happened if Aunt Ester were alive.

While Aunt Ester was alive, all alcohol was forbidden, and every Thanksgiving dinner at her house, a group of us dissenters would assemble with sweet tea in our glasses – but we were mad about it. We'd huddle together on the deck or front yard, just out of earshot from the matriarch, and together we'd dream about the day when prohibition would end on our corner of Knoxville, Tennessee.

It did. Wine was served the first Thanksgiving after Aunt Ester's funeral. That year, Thanksgiving was hosted by another member of the family who was excited to take up the mantle, and Aunt Janie was not a teetotaler. That gave some of us, not all, but many members of the extended family the chance to quietly sip from wine glasses at that first liberated Thanksgiving. I remember how we were whispering to one another, "This never would have happened if Aunt Ester were still around."

The next year, wine was served more openly, and by the third year everyone was just about comfortable. The fourth year after Aunt Ester's death, however, the invitation to this big Thanksgiving dinner for the whole extended family never came.

The host family needed a year off, so Aunt Janie asked that families celebrate their own Thanksgiving. A meal for all the cousins and everyone at her house was just too much.

We all understood. And we gave thanks in smaller numbers, around dining room tables in Atlanta, Washington DC, Knoxville, and Spartanburg, South Carolina, all looking forward to getting back together the next year. But another year passed, and then another without the invitation. Now, we don't even look for it. These days on Thanksgiving, we take the wine for granted, but we miss our extended family.

A Thanksgiving where we don't all get together would never have happened if Aunt Ester were still around.

Do you know this feeling? You're finally free to do what you want; only the freedom is not as wonderful as you thought it would be.

Maybe you've been like me, unsupervised at Home Depot, shopping for Christmas lights, buying without moderation, only to get home to wonder, "Where am I going to put all these Christmas lights?"

Freedom is not always what it's cracked up to be.

Hear again these words from the Prophet Isaiah: "O that you would tear open the heavens and come down. Because you hid yourself, we transgressed. We have all become like one who is unclean, and all our righteous deeds are like a filthy cloth."

What the Prophet means here is that without God, the people left unsupervised have so lost track of who they are that they call on God to return, even if it means punishment.

"Because you hid yourself, we transgressed."

"We have all become like one who is unclean, and all our righteous deeds are like a filthy cloth. We all fade like a leaf, and our iniquities, like the wind, take us away."

According to Isaiah we are all like kids who come home from school to an empty house with no one home. The computer is locked, but we figured out the password, and the liquor cabinet is locked too, but we've had enough time to find the key. No one is there to stop us.

As adults, we face the same problems with freedom - we spend what we want on credit cards sent in the mail. Because we've been given the freedom to take on debt we spend, even if the debt gets so deep we'll never emerge from it.

We eat what tastes best, forgetting the doctor's orders even when it jeopardizes our health.

We speak without thinking, act without thought to consequence. Sometimes when I read the headlines of the paper, it reminds me of that book I read in English Class years ago: *Lord of the Flies*. We have freedom, but Piggy's dead and we need some real grown-ups to save us from ourselves. We're losing decency and moderation. Even our leaders speak without thinking, take without asking, because no one is around to supervise us.

Maybe you saw the political cartoon in this morning's paper. "More Harassment Charges" is the headline, and the woman says to a friend, "I used to have coffee with my morning shows, popcorn with my movies ... now, I just eat Tums."

The Prophet cries out to God: "That you would tear open the heavens and come down, because you are the glue that holds us together and if you are gone then things fall apart."

"You hid yourself, and we transgressed because temptation is too much if you are not there to stop us."

"You have hidden your face from us and have delivered us into the hand of our iniquity." We have done all this – created a world of materialism where we all rush through giving thanks to get to spending more money than we have.

We work, and we work, and no one is there to tell us when to stop, so tension rises in our homes. There is no rest, even on the Sabbath, because who is there to speak over the loud voice of our culture that never stops telling us to produce and spend?

And so, we are entertained, but seldom happy.

Our bellies are full without ever being satisfied.

We keep going at a fool's pace, but where are we headed?

We have all become like one who is unclean, and all our righteous deeds are like a filthy cloth. We all fade like a leaf, and our iniquities, like the wind, take us away.

Deliver us Lord, from the hand of our iniquity.

"Come, Lord Jesus," we cry, for we are like grown children home from college, sleeping on God's couch, lulled into the illusion that we own the place and can do what we want. But He's coming back. We anticipate His birth during this season of Advent, preparing for His arrival as a precious mother's child.

May your prayer and mine this Advent Season be a simple one: "Restore us, O God; let Your face shine, that we may be saved [from ourselves]." And in His face, may we see the abundant life that can be ours.

Amen.

The Voice of One Crying Out in the Wilderness
Isaiah 40:1-11 and Mark 1:1-8

This has been an interesting weekend.

It snowed. It's the very thing we hope for in December, and after enjoying it for about two hours we wanted it to go away.

Isn't that funny?

But that's life.

This week got off to an interesting start for me. It had me really thinking.

Lily, Cece, and I were on our way to school Monday morning on our bikes, running a little behind before we had even made it out of the house. And you know how those mornings are – we were late, so we became later.

We were searching for all kinds of things! It was as though someone had sneaked into our house and hidden all the shoes and backpacks in places where we couldn't find them. So, after several delays, we finally made it down our steep driveway and were well on our way on our bikes when I realized that I was peddling but my wheels weren't moving.

I stopped to see if the chain was off, but it seemed as though my chain ring was no longer properly attached to the wheel. That was a problem, and this was one of those frustrating moments. We were already running late. My daughters were ahead of me – their peddles worked, you see – and so they had already made it across the street and were on their way around a corner. I didn't know what to do or how to catch up, and just then, Whitt Smith, who was a year ahead of me at Marietta High School, stopped in his pickup truck to say, "Ya'll are running a little late for school."

That was true, but it seemed like an obvious point to make.

I told him my bike wasn't working, and he told me to throw it in the back of his truck. He said that he'd drop it off back at our house. That way I could catch up with Lily and Cece and get them to school safely. I did, and we were only about 15 minutes late for school.

Under "reason for being tardy" I wrote "bike problems," and then wondered if anyone had ever thought up that excuse before. But here's the real question that I want you to ponder with me: on my walk from Westside Elementary School to the church, what will occupy my thoughts?

Will I spend this quiet time walking along the sidewalk stewing in the frustration from a malfunctioning bicycle – or, will I rejoice in thanksgiving for the kindness of an old friend who stopped to lend me a hand with my bike when I needed it?

It's been like this for me all weekend. Will I enjoy the snow for the rare gift that it is, or will my cheer be overcome by frustration because the power's out and I can't make coffee properly?

I can tell you how it's been for me – and I don't like it, for I'd much rather focus on how it was for our children who know how to enjoy a gift.

We adults don't always see things so well.

Snow looks like an inconvenience.

A friend's display of kindness gets lost amid frustration.

Miracles happen – but we don't always notice.

I'm afraid that it's always been this way. It's been this way since the beginning.

We just read the opening verses of the Gospel of Mark. The first line there is: "The beginning of the good news of Jesus Christ, the Son of God," and while this first line seems standard enough, consider all the other news that hit the papers that Monday morning 2,000 years ago competing for attention:

It was the beginning of the good news of Jesus Christ, the Son of God, but in addition to that, back in ancient Israel, Herod was the king, and his rule was oppressive and tyrannical. His primary concern was building palaces rather than establishing order and fairness.

In those days there was plenty of reason for good people to be consumed with hatred of the local government. Rome was the power that controlled the known world, and it maintained that control through public violence. Any who rose up in protest were nailed to crosses that lined the major roads into cities. These crosses were like our billboards. As you entered Jerusalem, they were your warning not to step out of line.

Think of that. This good news of Jesus Christ that the Gospel of Mark speaks of was first proclaimed in a time when most people believed there was only bad news.

Had we been there with them, we would have heard about the Good News among a chorus of government control, taxation, oppression, and poverty. Just as it has been true of us this weekend, that is how it has always been. It has always been a choice to hear the good news.

I said "choice." That's what I meant.

For the Good News is a light – but it's a light in the darkness.

It is a whisper in the cacophony of a city street.

The news is good – but it's good during bad times, so we must be practiced in how we listen and where we focus, because we must filter through all the chaos to get to the beauty and the truth.

Back in ancient Israel, in order to hear the Good News, some had to leave the city. They went out to a place where they could listen – they went out to the river to see John.

Did you catch those details about John from our second Scripture Lesson?

Clothed in camel's hair, with a leather belt around his waist, eating locusts and wild honey. Who looks like that? Who expects to be taken seriously looking like that?

I once had the chance to ask this big time, New York City preacher for advice. He looked me up and down and told me that I needed to shine my shoes.

That was it.

My confusion must have shown because he explained: "Presbyterians are respectable people who expect you to look like someone worth taking seriously." That's true. I know not to wear my Christmas suit in the pulpit on a Sunday morning, but what do we do with John?

What did he wear?

A business suit? No.

A robe? No.

Two articles of clothing did he wear: a camel hair something (and you can bet it wasn't a sport coat), then a belt. Nothing more. Why listen?

Because that's what prophets wear – that's why. Just because we're used to reading the news in the paper and hearing the news on TV, sometimes it's weird looking prophets from whom we hear the truth.

But that makes listening hard. That means discernment, because often it's lies coming through a bullhorn while the truth is proclaimed by a man dressed in camel hair.

We must learn how to listen – how to focus our attention, because we're distracted.

I saw a truck advertisement last week. Two little girls in the back seat looking at their iPad: "The new 2018 Ford F-150 with SYNC Connect and available Wi-Fi means you and the family can stay connected."

Connected?

What do we mean by connected?

How are we supposed to hear with all these distractions?

How are we supposed to be a family with all the entertainment?

Today is the Second Sunday of Advent, and today we are called on to consider peace, and to prepare for peace's coming in the birth of our Savior.

But how will we if we don't even know what being connected means anymore?

To start, I challenge you, as I challenge myself, to choose how you'll focus.

To watch for beauty, and to listen for truth.

A Bible scholar named Walter Brueggemann says it like this:

> *It is written in Deuteronomy that the poor will always be with you. It is written elsewhere that there will always be wars and rumors of wars. It is written in the American psyche that the big ones will always eat the little ones. It is written in the hearts of many hurting ones that their situation will always be abusive and exploitative. It is written, and it is believed, and it is lived, that the world is a hostile, destructive place. You must be on guard and maintain whatever advantage you can. It is written and recited like a mantra, world without end.*

[But] In the middle of that hopelessness, Advent issues a vision of another day, written by the poet, given to Israel midst the deathly cadence. We do not know when, but we know for sure. The poet knows for sure that this dying and killing is not forever, because another word has been spoken [but will hear it?][5]

There was a lady I once knew who was hard to visit because she never had anything nice to say. She was always sick, so I'd go to her home or to her hospital room. She was always cold, and in the summer time she'd bring a toboggan to wear in the sanctuary because she didn't like the air conditioning.

She was huddled up under blankets this one day I went to see her in her home, and she cried and cried telling me that no one from the church ever called, and that broke my heart to hear, but in that moment the phone rang. Doris from the church wanted to check and see how this lady was doing.

My mouth hung open because of the miracle, but this lady hung up the phone and said, "Where was I, oh yes – no one from the church ever calls me. It's horrible!"

It's like the hymn says:

And man, at war with man, hears not
The love song which they bring;
O hush the noise, ye men of strife,
And hear the angels sing.

They do sing, and they will sing, but we must be quiet and calm enough to listen.

We must be careful about what we pay attention to.

And we must watch our hearts – because you and I can stew all day long on what doesn't matter ultimately while ignoring the miracles.

They are like the voice of one crying out in the wilderness.

Listen – because that's hope calling.

Amen.

---

[5] Walter Brueggemann, *Devotions for Advent: Celebrating Abundance* (Westminster John Knox Press, Louisville, 2017) 10.

The One Who Can Turn on the Lights
Genesis 1:1-5 and John 1:1-9

Every night our girls humor me by asking me to tell them a story. Last Monday night, Lily wanted to hear a story about when I was her age. I told her about how when I was 8 years old, my favorite school lunch at Hickory Hills Elementary School was something called a taco boat.

You might remember those things. The taco shells were flat, but pulled up on the edges like a square corn piecrust. The lunch ladies would scoop taco beef into them, then lettuce and salsa. I remember all that because this was my favorite school lunch, and talking about these taco boats reminded me of one day when I was going through the lunch line with my best friend Matt Buchanan.

I was new at Hickory Hills in third grade (Lily's age), and Matt was in third grade too, but he had been at the school longer, so he was kind of showing me the ropes. We were going through the line, and right before we got to the cash register, he said, "Watch this."

Lunch was 85 cents in those days, and Matt pulled out a dollar, handed it to the lady, and said to her, "Keep the change." Then, with a wink, he walked to our table.

I thought this was the coolest thing I had ever seen. It was like going through the lunch line with James Dean or something. So, I took out my dollar and handed it to the lady. "Keep the change," I said, but she handed me back my 15 cents.

The moral of the story: some people have it and some people don't. That's just the way it is.

Sometimes you just must stay in your lane, and Matt Buchanan was the Fonz of Hickory Hills. I was lucky to be his less cool sidekick, which was fine, because you must know who you are – and you must know who you are not.

I'm not Matt.

I'm also not Sara.

There was a month when Sara asked me to take over paying the bills for our family. She gave me instructions with all the passwords, and it was still the most stressful month of my life.

127

She's also whom the girls want when they're sick – unless there's throw-up involved. That's me.

And when we all leave the house in the morning, Lily and Cece both say, "I love you Mama. You're the best Mom ever."

They love me too, I know that, but there's something about a mom. That's just how it is, and that's fine with me because it's good to know who I am and who I'm not. There's freedom in coming to terms with that, and there's suffering if you never do – so it is with some joy that I say, "I'm just Joe." Not Matt, not Sara, and not Jesus either. And while that last one may sound the most obvious of all, I'm not the only mortal who often attempts to live up to immortal standards. I'm not the only human who has trouble accepting the reality of his human-ness. Consider just the last two campaign slogans for President of the United States.

I'm not trying to make a particularly political statement. I just want to say this morning that all those supporters who believe that President Trump is powerful enough to go right up to Washington and "Make America Great Again" are going to be disappointed, because no mortal can do it – especially not on his own.

But this is politics.

Human politicians promise the impossible. They say they can do these things, which they can't, and we are fools to believe them.

You remember President Obama's campaign slogan? "Hope."

No human should promise that, because hope is not ours.

We mortals must come to terms with mortality.

We must understand the limits of our power.

We must know who we are and who we are not. And that's why it's important that we go back to the river this morning – back to the Jordan River to visit John for the second Sunday in a row.

And who is John?

There's some descriptive information about him in our Second Scripture Lesson, but this passage gives us mostly a description of who he is not: "There was a man sent from God, whose name was John. He came as a witness to testify to the light, so that all might believe through him. He himself was not the light, but he came to testify to the light. The true light, which enlightens everyone, was coming into the world."

So, who's John? He's not the light and he knew it.

A preacher and Bible Scholar named David Bartlett said it like this: "What Would Jesus do?" the button asks. "He would walk on water, give sight to the blind, and raise the dead."

We must know who we are not – and who we are not is the Light of the world.

That sounds obvious enough, but it's not. Or it's not for me anyway.

Last Sunday I was nervous, and it was because I was confused about my limits. I was thinking all Saturday after we'd made the decision not to cancel this worship service that if our people are going to go through all the trouble of getting here on a snow day, I better have a pretty good sermon.

That might be true, but you're not here for me. If I spend all this time pointing to myself, if this church becomes all about me or you or anyone else, if the focus of our attention is on what any mortal has to say and think and do, then we are a shell of the church that we could be. Because it's not me or my words that matter. It's whom I'm talking about.

It's whom they're singing about.

It's whom we're praying to.

It's whom we honor and thank with our tithes and offerings.

The focus of our praise must never be on a mortal. For it is the call of us humans to use our words and actions to point to the One who spoke light into the world.

A great theologian, some would say the greatest of the 20th Century, was a man named Karl Barth. From 1921 until his death, over his desk hung a copy of a painting by Matthias Grunewald. In the center of the painting hangs Christ crucified, and to one side stands John the Baptist – one hand raised and pointing to the Light of the World.

"There was a man sent from God, whose name was John. He came as a witness to testify to the light. He himself was not the light," and what we can learn from John is that John the Baptist knew he wasn't.

He knew himself well enough that he knew who he was and the gifts that God had given him. He used those gifts so well because he pointed to someone worth pointing to. He is, therefore, the very definition of humble.

The definition of humble is simple. It's knowing what you can do and what you can't do, who you are and who you are not. John was a messenger, not the Light itself. We can learn a lot from just that.

After all, this is a time of year when everyone is going overboard. Doing too much. Attempting to make real the impossible. Trying to make someone's dreams come true. This time of year, we forget who we are and who we are not, and that leads to doomed expectations.

Grandma died, so someone is going to try to make macaroni and cheese just like she always made it. But even if it's perfect, we can't bring Grandma back.

And last Christmas, Charlie was disappointed, so someone here is going to find the perfect thing in the perfect size but listen – be realistic – you can't buy joy. You just can't.

Even if this Christmas you were to wake up to a Lexus in your driveway with a big red bow on it, you've still shot for the moon without reaching it. That's because you can't be hope, you can't be Christmas Joy, and you can't be the Light of the World. And if we're busy trying to be that, not only are we doomed to frustration, but we're missing out on the blessings that our God longs to give by trying to provide them for ourselves.

We're trying to scrape by on our own while He promises abundant life.

We're trying to fill the table for a feast, but He's the one who turns water into wine.

And maybe we've thrown some Christmas lights on the tree, but He's the Light of the World.

A preacher named Bob Woods tells a story about the light in a cave.

This couple took their son and daughter to Carlsbad Caverns. The tour of this cave is like a lot of them. The guide takes you way down there, to the cave's deepest point underground, and then turns off the lights, just to show how dark darkness can be.

Enveloped in complete darkness, the little boy began to cry.

Immediately was heard the quiet voice of his sister who said, "Don't cry. Someone here knows how to turn on the lights."

You see — this time of year we're busy talking about remembering Grandma through the perfect replication of her macaroni and cheese, while Jesus is coming to make the dead alive.

We're busy searching the Internet for the greatest gift money can buy, while Jesus is born bringing hope to the world.

And up in Washington D.C. they're doing very mortal things while promising what only God can give — so do not be deceived. Do not be frustrated. Instead, look to the Manger because the one who knows how to turn on the lights is coming.

Our Clerk of Session, Carol Calloway, and I were texting back and forth last Saturday trying to decide what to do about opening the church. I asked her if she had power back yet and she wrote me back, "I am very aware of where our real power comes from." Being without power makes that obvious.

My friends, there are limits to human power, but rejoice in this: The One who knows how to turn on the lights is coming to be with us.

Amen.

How Can This Be?
2 Samuel 7:1-11, 16 and Luke 1:26-38

I've just read you two Scripture Lessons where things don't go according to the plans – not according to the human plans, that is. That's good, because today is a day for coming to terms with the reality that even the best laid plans of mice and men often go astray.

Think about it. Today is the kind of day where we cook turkeys, entertain guests, and open presents with certain expectations in mind, while getting the National Lampoon's Christmas Vacation version instead.

You remember how Aunt Bethany wrapped up her cat?

You were hoping for an instapot, but you might wind up surprised, for even while we hope for a perfect Christmas, we must remember the lesson taught by movies like *The Best Christmas Pageant Ever:* it was the best because as everything went wrong, as everything planned fell apart, it finally became clear what really matters.

But that's a hard lesson. To live such a lesson requires a depth of spiritual discipline ... a readiness to surrender our will to the will of the Divine. Scripture offers us two examples to learn from this morning – one of a king, the other of a virgin, both of whom wrestle with God in accepting that their plans will not come to fruition because God has a greater plan in mind.

Consider King David with me. There in 2 Samuel we see that he wants to build God a house. The problem is that God doesn't want a house.

This kind of thing is common enough – for sometimes the giver wants to give what the receiver would prefer not to receive. So, David settles into his house and realizes his fortune, but upon realizing his fortune he worries about God and says to the great Prophet Nathan: "See now, I am living in a house of cedar, but the ark of God stays in a tent."

He's being thoughtful here but being thoughtful isn't always enough.

Say you buy yourself a nice chainsaw for Christmas and enjoy it so much that you buy one for your wife. The only problem is that your wife doesn't want a chainsaw – unless she's Sandra Brice, that is – for the giver must recognize that his wants might not be the same as his spouse's.

132

Aunt Clara made Ralphie a pink bunny suit that he hated. For years our grandmother would buy these great, big, poppy seed muffins from Sam's for my sister Elizabeth, until finally, after choking them down Christmas after Christmas, she finally said, "But Nanny, I don't really like those things."

Well, God, upon hearing David's plan, goes to the Prophet Nathan and says, "Go and tell my servant David: 'Thus, says the Lord: Are you the one to build me a house to live in? I have not lived in a house since the day I brought up the people of Israel from Egypt to this day... and I have been with you wherever you went.'"

It's as though God is saying: "You want me to live in a house? But I'd much rather stay with you." And which one is better? Wouldn't we all rather have God live in our hearts than in some big, cold, stone temple? Of course we would – and that's what God wants too. After all, this is the day when we celebrate the truth that rather than dwell up in Heaven or be confined to a house, the Lord is born, flesh and blood, to dwell among us. However, for David to see the glory of this gift he must get over the disappointment that his plan won't happen right away.

Today is a day for coming to terms with reality – for in life, even some of our best-laid plans never come to fruition because God has better ones.

But we don't always like that.

Think about the new car you bought. How good it smelled, how well it ran, how it stretched your budget just a little too far. But you loved it, and then your family piles in and one of them throws up in the back seat.

You know what I'm talking about. This is frustrating. We make these plans, set up these expectations, and when they fall apart, we are so often blind to the blessing that rises from the rubble.

We wanted to build God a house, but God wants to dwell with us – isn't that wonderful?

It is wonderful. If you can see it, that is. Seeing something like that is hard. And imagine how hard it would have been for Mary.

I can imagine the plan Mary had dreamed up for herself.

She was engaged to Joseph, and surely in the weeks and months leading up to her wedding she'd imagined how she'd be the center of attention.

All the talk where the women were washing clothes would be about what she would wear.

The vendors at the market place would stop her to make suggestions for what should be served.

Her younger sisters were jealous that their time had not yet come.

Her aunts were envious because theirs had already passed.

And Mary was simultaneously impatiently looking forward to the day and wanting there to be just a little more time to get those tablescapes in order (I bet you didn't expect me to know that word – I learned it in a magazine that I'll tell you about later. But now back to Mary).

Mary would be the bride – she knew that on her big day all eyes would be on her - she would be beautiful, and everything would be perfect. It would be her day, and this day of hers would lead to years of happiness.

There would be a new home and it would be hers.

There would be children to fill it up in time.

Plus, all the while this man, Joseph, who adored her would be there and they would build this life together.

It was a beautiful plan that surely Mary had laid out in her mind, and I don't believe that Mary asks for too much. Certainly, there is nothing here that she doesn't deserve, but God had another plan.

The angel said to her, "Do not be afraid, Mary, for you have found favor with God. And now, you will conceive in your womb and bear a son, and you will name him Jesus. He will be great and will be called the Son of the Highest, and the Lord God will give to him the throne of his ancestor David. He will reign over the house of Jacob forever, and of his kingdom there will be no end."

Now this plan sounds good. In fact, it is so good that we call it the Greatest Story Ever Told. For 2,000 years we've been calling this plan the Good News. The only problem is that it wasn't Mary's plan. In fact, the plan that the angel Gabriel presents may well guarantee that Mary's plan never happens.

It's true.

A pregnant bride? The wedding will not be a celebration anymore but a scandal. That's if it even happens, because what will Joseph think? Mary would have known that it would be within his rights to have her stoned, so this plan of Gabriel's may lead to Mary's death.

Think about that.

For when we come face to face with such disappointment, when our best laid plans don't just change or get postponed but turn to tragedy, how can we not despair? Mary on the other hand can be our example this Christmas, for even as her expectations fall apart, she sees blessing.

Mary hears this angelic announcement, this declaration that God intends to derail her plans completely, and still says, "Here am I, the servant of the Lord; let it be with me according to your word."

She is God's favored one, not because she laid out her plans perfectly, but because she was willing to say "yes" to plans that were not her own. She could see that God was at work when everything changed and when everything seemed to have changed for the worst, but would you and I have had the faith to believe it?

In some ways, I'm sure we all already do.

When it comes right down to it, I also know that not everything good that I have in my life is there because I knew I wanted it. In fact, the very best things in my life came not because I chose them, but because they chose me.

That's a reality of life, I believe. The destination that you choose may not be the best destination. The life that you think you want may not in fact be the life that will make you happy. And all the best Christmas memories come, not as a result of good planning and the execution of an ideal plan – instead, it's like the movies have taught us, the best Christmas memories so often come when everything goes the opposite of the way you want them to.

As I said before, I learned about tablescapes because I had the occasion to leaf through Paula Deen's Christmas magazine. Don't ask me why. In it are recipes, gift ideas, instructions for wrapping presents, and pictures of her tablescapes. For brunch on Christmas day Paula suggests that you "create a serene setting for a morning gathering fashioned with hues of green and a variety of earthy textures. Delicious offerings of baked eggs and grits, maple-glazed skewers, and cream cheese and cranberry baked French toast will bring the event to life."[6] But I assure you, it's not the cranberry baked French toast that would bring this event to life - it's the children who will climb from their high chairs and booster seats to throw every element of that tablescape of earthy textures to the floor.

So, while it's good to figure out an image and a plan for the perfect Christmas and it's good to aspire to Paula Deen's standards, I want you to know that in Paula Deen's magazine there is no one seated at that perfect Christmas Day table. How could there be? For it's not the turkey that came out perfect that I will always remember, but the Christmas turkey Uncle Al cooked with the bag of giblets still in it.

I hope you have a plan and that you'll go after it. But before you get too stuck in your plans, remember that true fulfillment may lie, not in your intended destination, but in another place you never dreamed you'd go.

And while we tend to think about celebrating Christmas with the perfect Christmas dinner, that's hardly what this day is about – for Christ comes to change the world.

Don't worry then about the flaw in what you'd hoped would be a perfect Christmas Card – for that's not what this is about. Today is about the God who comes incarnate, to cover not just our imperfections, but to set us free from pretending that we have it all together.

We think that this season is all about a moment when all is right with the world – when the fire crackles and everyone's happy – but you'll have to aim higher to even see what God intends, for He is coming to make things right, not just for a moment, but forever and ever.

Amen.

---

[6] Paula Deen. *Christmas: Serving up Family Traditions*, 71.

Living in the Fields
Isaiah 9:2-7 and Luke 2:1-14

I've been thinking so much about coal lately.

That isn't a particularly good thing to be thinking about. In fact, anyone mentioning coal on a night like tonight might make some children very worried – but I had a thought about coal. I've only ever heard of one child receiving coal on Christmas. He's grown now, and he is here in this room, and because I heard about it as a child the threat of coal was always very real. This year however, I had a new thought about coal.

A couple of weeks ago when it snowed and the power was out in our home for 24 hours, the house got cold, which made me mean.

It's true – it was so cold it made me grouchy. It was like the cold shrunk my heart so that it was two sizes too small, and I was on edge. My wife Sara was too, and we found ourselves aggravated at each other over tiny things. It was awful, and so later it occurred to me that perhaps Santa brings bad children coal because it is impossible to be good if you're cold.

Now some don't know that coal has anything to do with heat, but do you remember that furnace in the basement of Ralphie's house in *A Christmas Story?* How the black smoke comes out from the coal burning down there? Ralphie's dad goes down to fix it, and as he's down there banging around, narrator Ralphie says: "In the heat of battle, my father wove a tapestry of obscenity, that as far as we know is still hanging in space over Lake Michigan." Maybe that furnace didn't always work, but at least they had one. And what if that yellow eyed bully Scut Farcus didn't?

Maybe he was just mean, or maybe he was just cold. It's hard to be good when you're cold.

It's hard to be good when you always get a cold shoulder too.

Years ago, I had just graduated from college with a major in religion. If there are any college students out there, let me steer you towards the study of a more marketable subject that this one that I chose, because after graduation and before I started seminary, the only job I could get was cutting grass for a company called Habersham Gardens in Atlanta.

I had a driver's license, which worked in my favor, and I was quickly promoted to truck driver. I remember how even at Christmas time there were leaves to

137

blow and grass to cut, because this is Georgia. So, there I was, standing by the truck when the homeowner was walking into the house with her two children. She speaks to us, but as she was just out of our earshot, I heard her say, "That's why you go to college kids – so you don't have to do that for a living."

"Merry Christmas to you too lady," is what I wanted to say, because getting the cold shoulder can make you mean. But I kept silent. I had learned my place as so many do. In a culture of sinful humans there are those who live in the nice big houses and there are those who work outside of them.

There are those who buy the Christmas Trees and there are those who sell them.

There are those who work in the offices and those who clean them.

There are those who drive the cars and there are those who park them.

And the worst part is that if we get the cold shoulder too often, we don't just get mad, we get broken.

We start to imagine that some matter more, or that some count but we don't.

Maybe we start to imagine that some people are worthy of the good life and that we're not.

We give up on the privileges and settle in out in the cold.

That's right – even on Christmas Eve there are those gathered by the fire and there are those who are out watching their flocks by night, and I wonder which one you feel like.

Shepherds are the focus of our Scripture Lesson from the Gospel of Luke. They were out in the fields, probably cold, and probably used to getting the cold shoulder too, because being a shepherd is and was a low-ranking job in most places. While Janie Harrison and a flock of kids donned bathrobes and held crooks this afternoon to play the shepherd part in the Christmas pageant, not a one of them smelled like a real shepherd would have.

Shepherds smell like sheep.

In those days, they slept outside, and some still do today.

They didn't live in the cities, but out in the fields, and they weren't part of the respected class, because they weren't respected. In fact, back in the time of the

Christmas Story, well to do people placed statues of shepherds in the gardens because they were the class of people it was OK to make fun of.

The way that we have statues of jockeys out in front of our houses or gnomes in the garden – if conversation lagged during a garden party back in those days a wealthy person might point out her host's shepherd statue to make a joke, "He's missing more teeth than he has."

If Jeff Foxworthy were around in the time of Jesus, he might have made a living telling shepherd jokes:

"If your grandmother's beard is more impressive than Santa's, you might be a shepherd.

If you have a deer stand in your Christmas tree, you might be a shepherd.

If you really do ask Santa for your two front teeth, you might be a shepherd."

This was an age of severe hierarchies of power and class, and we read there in verse 8 of chapter 2, "In that region there were shepherds *living* in the fields." Not in houses – in fields.

So, how then did they smell?

Who did their laundry?

What did they eat?

And who took the time to see them as children of God?

That's who they were, but shepherds had many opportunities to forget that, many chances to believe that they deserved the disrespect that they received day after day. But then one night God showed up and told them who they truly were.

God stopped to tell them, before anyone else, that his Son was born in Bethlehem.

Do you know the difference that this can make?

When someone stops and sees you, really sees you, on a cold night when you feel invisible?

I do, because some have made this kind of difference to me. I was a college student several years ago, and on the day of a test in a class on the Old Testament, I thought it prudent to wear roller blades. I rolled right to my desk, sat down, made a D, and was called up to my professor's office the next week.

Dr. Peter Hobbie is his name, and he asked me to sit, then looked me in the eye and asked, "Joe Evans, when are you going to start taking yourself seriously?"

You know there are moments in life when things change. When you see yourself differently because someone finally saw you differently. When you take yourself seriously, because someone believes that you are worth taking seriously. When he looks, not down his nose at you but right into your eyes and sees in you something that you have never seen in yourself, because for so long you've felt passed over, ignored, or left behind.

Do you know the enormity of being seen? Of being spoken to?

Just a few words, but everything changes.

That's what the angel did to these shepherds.

God's angel spoke saying, "To you is born this day in the city of David a Savior, who is the Messiah, the Lord."

"To you," the angel said. Not to the lady who used you to teach her children a lesson – no, to you. For the truth is that you're precious, valued, and honorable, regardless of the state of your clothes or your station. This angel told them, "To you is born this day in the city of David a Savior, who is the Messiah, the Lord," and when they heard this news, they didn't stop to take a shower and change their clothes. They went with haste and found Mary and Joseph and the child lying in the manger.

Consider that. Consider how God changed them with a few simple words. But that is exactly what God does – and listen – God is doing it again tonight.

Whether you're a shepherd out in a field, a mother in a suburb, or a businessman with a briefcase, this world of ours has a way of breaking us down without ever building us back up. But listen – one voice can change all that. Or better yet – one birth can change all that by waking you and me up to the truth of who we are.

As the angels said it to the shepherds – know that they say the same to you: "Do not be afraid, for see – I am bringing you good news of great joy for all

140

the people. To you is born this day in the city of David a Savior, who is the Messiah, the Lord."

Glory to God in the highest heaven,

And on earth peace among you – whom He favors.

Amen.

Part 5

The Season after Christmas

Just as our Christmas Trees must be swept away before New Year's Day in an abrupt and sudden change, so from accounts of the baby Jesus in the season of Christmas, scripture jumps to His baptism and His calling of the first disciples.

The following are sermons on those events early in the ministry of our Lord.

Into What Then Were You Baptized
Genesis 1:1-5 and Mark 1:4-11

Some would say that the hardest words to believe in the Bible are those in our First Scripture Lesson:

In the beginning, when God created the heavens and the earth, the earth was a formless void and darkness covered the face of the deep… Then God said, let there be light.

Science tells us a story about a big bang and an ever-expanding universe, survival of the fittest, and natural selection. For generations now, it's as though faith and science have been battling it out for a right to the truth.

Like me you might say that there is no either or, but maybe you've had an argument with your friends about this issue. Some friend might see the first two chapters of Genesis as the great stumbling block that keeps them from faith in God – but I say these words in Genesis are no stumbling block. They don't need to compete with the words of science, because science can tell us things that religion never will. Scripture provides insights that science cannot, but beyond that, these scriptural words from Genesis aren't the hardest words to believe anyway. No. If you get right down to it, most people wrestle not with the words of our first scripture lesson, but the words of our second: "It was just as He was coming up out of the water, when a voice came from Heaven saying, 'You are my Son, the Beloved; with You I am well pleased.' "

Most people can't believe that God or anyone else would ever say that to them.

"You are my daughter, whom I love, and with you I am well pleased."

"You are my son, whom I love; with you I am well pleased."

"You are my husband or my wife, whom I love, and with you I am well pleased."

These words are common enough, but they're also different from what we're used to hearing. It might sound normal enough were God to say to Jesus or to us, "I have high hopes for who you might become." It might sound normal enough were God to say, "Now, once all the laundry is washed," or "When you get that raise so we can put a pool in the back yard, then I'll really be impressed."

Rather, what God is saying to Jesus in His baptism is, ""It's because of who You are right now that I just have to say, "You are Mine. You are the One I love, and with You I am well pleased.""

I know a woman who went on a date set up by one of those matchmaker websites. This guy said to her: "You have the exact skill set that I've been looking for in a partner."

That's not very romantic. It sounds more like engineering than love to me, but we hear those kinds of words so often that not all of us are able to let the Good News in.

We're not used to the truth that in our baptism, what God said to Jesus, God says to us all, as well.

That in baptism, God takes us as His own.

God loves us as His own.

God claims us as His own.

With us ... even with us ... God is well pleased.

As Presbyterians, we baptize infants, and we need to stop and think about what that means. What has a four-month-old done to qualify for these words?

Nothing. But that's grace. That's God's love, and considering Jesus in the Gospel of Mark, even for Jesus it's not so different for Him than it is for an infant. This morning we read from Chapter 1 of Mark's gospel – the very first chapter. No miracles precede this baptism. He doesn't say anything wise to please God, making Him deserving of this affirmation. Instead, Jesus just walks into the water, and God speaks these most important words because that's what baptism is. It is undeserved grace and love that some struggle to accept for their entire lives.

Like us, He is a child of God. But unlike us, when God tells Him so, He is bold to believe it.

Like us, God who holds the whole world in His hands also holds tightly this Jesus of Nazareth. But unlike us, Jesus never doubts it.

Like us, Jesus hears this Good News, that God is well pleased with who He is. But unlike us, these words free Him from shame.

"You are Mine, My beloved, and with You I am well pleased." Jesus heard these words. He never doubted them. Even as God called Him to face the cross, still He knew who He was. Still He knew that He was beloved of God. But can you and I let these words in?

There's a power in words. That's the difference between the Creation account in Genesis and the story science tells. It's not that one is right and one is wrong – it's that science tells us that it's all about molecules and energy, and that's fine and good, but none of that matters to your soul nearly as much as words do. So, in Genesis God spoke and there was light.

That's the truth. And you know it is, because it's not photons but words that bring light to so much of the darkness that we know. Some never hear those words and others can't believe them. Isn't that the truth?

The 17th Century poet George Herbert in his third poem titled "Love" wrote: "Love bade me welcome, but my soul drew back." That seems to be the natural human reaction.

Valentine's Day is coming up, and over the years I've read a lot of children's books about Valentine's Day from the library. They're all just about the same. In everyone a little girl sends a valentine card to a little boy, then on the playground or somewhere, she sneaks up behind him and plants a kiss on his cheek. 100% of the time – in every one of those books - the little boy runs away. Little boys are funny about love.

It was when I was in second grade that my teacher asked our class to go home and ask our parents about what is essential for life. It was science class and we were learning about what it takes to survive. My parents and I decided on water. Water is essential for life, I reported to my class. I was proud to find that this was a good and acceptable answer. "Yes, water is essential for life," our teacher responded. Then a girl in the class answered oxygen, which was also a good answer. Then another said food. The teacher approved and said that food is also essential for life.

A boy in the row behind me reported that love was essential for life.

I couldn't get my head around that, so I went home and asked my Mom. She agreed with the boy and told me that no one could live without love, which didn't make any sense to me at the time. So, I went to my father and he told me that the boy's parents must be hippies.

Love. It's essential, but sometimes it's easier to joke about. So, the poem from George Herbert continues:

Love bade me welcome: yet my soul drew back...
But quick-eyed Love, observing me grow slack...
Drew nearer to me, sweetly questioning
If I lacked anything.

The poet answers: *I lack what would make me worthy.*

There's the real challenge. Like the poet we say: "Surely, I'm not worthy of love. I should have to pay for it, work for it, aspire to one day deserve it." But what if it's just like the Gospel of Mark says it is? What if all you have do is come up from the water and hear the words?

Words are powerful. God speaks them, and the earth is created. And God speaks them in baptism. By those words our lives are changed completely if we'll let the power of the words do their work.

So, if your earthly father never said them, or never said them enough, then hear them said to you by your Heavenly Father: "You are mine."

Or if you've struggled to believe them, because love showed up and then walked away, know that the God who came to earth to say them through His life isn't going anywhere, least of all away from you: "You are Mine, My beloved."

The God of love ... He came to earth, and when He came up out of the water, He heard these words and He let them in. And for the rest of His life, He poured these words out, saying to His disciples, "Take and eat. This is My body broken for you. Drink. Here is My love poured out for you to take in. You are Mine, My beloved, and with you I am well pleased."

May these words free you to stop working so hard to deserve them, because you can't succeed.

May these words free you to be yourself, for until you can, you'll never be satisfied.

And may these words create in you a desire for new life, because we can't be saved from our sin until we accept the truth that we are worth saving.

Amen.

Come and See
1 Samuel 3:1-10 and John 1:43-51

Can anything good come out of Nazareth?

Can anything good come out of Nazareth?

What a question. What a human question – and what a relevant question for us to ponder this Sunday morning.

You and I know already that Scripture speaks truth to our world. We get out of bed Sunday after Sunday to hear it. We put the pulpit right here in the center of this great, revered room we call the Great Hall because the Word that Scripture reveals we put right at the center of our lives. That's why the Beadle carries the Bible in with dignity and respect, because the Beadle knows as we all know that the Bible is not some dusty book passed down from generation to generation, but the most relevant book that we could possibly read.

But who would have thought that this book, so ancient and removed from 21st Century America, would lead us to ponder a phrase nearly the same as a statement the President is reputed to have made just a few days ago?

Nathanial asks, "Can anything good come out of Nazareth?" And allegedly, asks the President, "Can anything good come out of a place like Haiti? Can anything good come out of Africa? Isn't it true that the best people come from Norway or someplace like that?"

Those aren't the words exactly, but you've watched the news and heard all about it. Regardless of exactly what was said and by whom, this is a very human assumption. We all try to get to know people and one of the very first questions we ask is, "Where are you from?" as though that could tell us something.

My grandfather came from a place called the Caw-Caw Swamp. I've never been there, but he'd tell us these stories of how they'd catch turtles and would fatten them up in copper pots before cooking them for dinner. He'd tell how the teacher would come to the house before his school was built, and there was a door to the front that only the teacher could use. Then he told us that when the school was built, my grandfather was the oldest school age child, so he was chosen to drive the bus. How old was he? "Oh, 12 at least", I remember his saying.

One day he fell asleep on his desk and some kid dropped a BB in his ear, and the story goes that because of the damage done to his eardrum he was never again allowed to swim.

I told Dr. Jim Goodlet the story and he told me that a BB should just fall back out again, because a BB is likely too big to do any real damage considering how narrow the ear canal is in a little boy. But the thing is, Jim is a real doctor, and who knows what kind of medical help my grandfather saw out in the Caw-Caw Swamp?

The first time he went to the beach, he told me he fully expected to look right across the water to see Europe, which doesn't speak too highly for his school system. As he started out in business in the nearest city, which was Charleston, South Carolina, who knows how many people looked down their noses at him when he told them he was from the Caw-Caw Swamp?

I can't tell you exactly where the Caw-Caw Swamp is, but it is not South of Broad.

People think that where you live really means something, so they ask about where you're from to learn about who you are. And that can be good. But to really get to know someone you must do something more. You must go deeper.

I've been interested to know how strategic some people are about using their Kroger Fuel Points. I ran into Wilkie Schell as I was dropping the girls off at school. They've so kindly allowed us to park in their driveway, which is right across the street from the school, and Wilkie told me he was checking the gas levels in both of their cars, because Libba and Wilkie wait until both cars are on empty before they go to gas up, so that they maximize their fuel savings at the Kroger.

Amazing.

I've been to a Christmas Party where the conversation completely revolved around tips for gaining a greater discount at the Kroger gas pumps. That tells you something about a person, though I'm not sure what.

Getting to know people.

Getting to really know people: How do you do it?

We once rented a house from a man named Greg Martin who later told me that he always made a point of looking inside a person's car before renting him or her a house. That, for him, was a good way of getting to know someone.

So, if you want to know someone, how clean is his car?

How much do they care about Kroger Fuel Points?

I'll tell you this: you learn more when you know the answer to either of those questions than when all you know is where a person came from.

I was in New York City one summer. I told a man I was from Georgia and he said, "I know."

A friend of mine is named Will. He's a Presbyterian minister down in Savannah. He went to a boarding school up North and when his roommate learned he was from Tennessee, he was surprised that Will owned shoes.

You ask someone where they're from, and what do you learn? Maybe nothing.

But what do you assume? A lot.

You remember *Hee Haw*? Grandpa comes down stairs: "Well everybody. I'm getting old. It's time for me to move up North."

"Why Grandpa?" everyone wants to know.

"I figure it's coming close to my time to leave this earth, and it's better if we lose one of them than one of us," he said.

Philip says to Nathaniel, "We have found Him about whom Moses in the law and the prophets wrote, Jesus, son of Joseph from Nazareth."

Nathaniel asked him, "Can anything good come out of Nazareth?"

Stop and listen to that. We think we can learn something about someone based on how long his or her family has lived here or whether they're from Cherokee or Paulding County. But take note: Jesus the Messiah comes from one of those places that people make assumptions about.

However, where He was from didn't tell Nathaniel anything because getting to know people, and I mean really getting to know them, can be valuable and life giving, but it isn't easy. It's not easy because you must turn off the part of your brain that relies on assumptions and operates on fear.

If you really want to get to know someone, you must do more. You must move in next door.

Here in Marietta, we live close to our neighbors, and this new proximity has made us aware of how loud we are. We have two dogs, and one day I opened the back door to tell one of them to stop barking, only to hear our next-door neighbor yelling: "Junebug, be quiet!"

It's bad when they know your dog's name, but unfortunately, or fortunately, our neighbors don't just know us, they really know us. And that's what it takes. To really get to know someone you must be around them. You must know what they eat and where they sleep. You must see what they're like when no one is looking or when they think no one is looking. The Gospel of John begins like this, as Eugene Peterson translated it: "The Word became flesh and blood and moved into the neighborhood."

That's what the Lord did – He moved into the neighborhood.

He didn't rely on assumptions or operate on fear. Out of love He came down here to really get to know us. That's who God is: A Creator who longs to know His creation.

To use the words from our Call to Worship, quoted from Psalm 139: "O Lord, you have searched me and known me. You know when I sit down and when I rise; you discern my thoughts from far away. You are acquainted with all my ways."

God was acquainted with Nathaniel, having knit him together in his mother's womb. But more than that, the Lord saw him underneath the fig tree.

Do you know what that feels like?

You leave a message on someone's voicemail, but instead of hanging up properly like you thought you did at the end of your brief message, you start in on your husband once again and the true state of your marriage is preserved on someone's cell phone.

Or maybe you were in the middle of a sensitive conversation in the kitchen when your daughter barges in. You don't know how long she's been listening or what all she heard, but you wish that the words that just spilled out of your mouth could be sucked back in.

It's a strange thing to know that you've been seen. It's intimate and makes you feel vulnerable. To be known is this incredible thing, but this is God's reality and we are wise to remember it. God sees so much that we would rather hide.

God knows us at this deep and substantial level.

All that we would deny or run away from, He sees and knows. But here's the big deal: Even in knowing all of that, He comes to earth to get to know us even better. Then — and this is the big news — even after seeing us for who we really are — God invites us to take part in what God is doing.

You can see what an honor this is. What a difference this kind of invitation makes in peoples' lives!

Did you see that picture of a Haitian born cadet who wept as he graduated from West Point?

Or did you hear about the boy who grew up in the Caw Caw Swamp to set records in insurance sales for Life of Georgia?

Then there's the kid who was left at a Temple by his mother, raised by a blind old man, bullied by the man's two sons, but was awakened in the middle of the night because God wanted Samuel to crown Israel's greatest kings.

We are all Nathaniels. We look down on others because we fear we are nothing ourselves.

Forget all that.

Let me tell you the truth. You might have come from some place that presidents and disciples would call a backwater place or worse, but you are precious in His sight. And, God has some work for you to do.

God sees in you the potential that no one else ever saw.

God sees the worth that you long ago forgot all about.

God knows when you are sleeping, and He knows when you're awake. And the greatest gift He could give, He has given. And the most important news He entrusts to you so that you might proclaim it. Just come and see.

Just come and see who you really are.

Just come and see, and take part in the redeeming work that God is doing in our world.

Amen.

Mending the Nets
Jonah 3:1-5 and Mark 1:14-20

This has been a big weekend at the church.

Yesterday was the church officers' retreat. Your elected Elders and Deacons were here. We were talking about the future of our church with excitement, moving forward into this new year, and in addition to all of that, in Holland Hall yesterday was the Cub Scout's Pinewood Derby.

I remember being a Cub Scout in Holland Hall for the Pinewood Derby. The scene was just about the same as it was yesterday. There was a long track. It used to be wood, but now it's metal. The cars line up in heats, and the Cub Scouts still all huddle around the starting line, cheering for these cars that they either made by themselves or with a parent.

Two of Judy and Bob Harper's grandsons are in our Cub Scout Troop and we were standing together with their son-in-law Rob. I asked Rob about the construction of his son's cars: "How much of that Pinewood Derby car are you responsible for?" He was telling me about how the boys did some of the sanding, but as for sawing the wood, he did most of that. At that point in the conversation, the father in front of us turned back and said, "Really, it all depends on whether you want to make a trip to the ER."

This is still the same.

When it comes to the Pinewood Derby, there's often that balance between letting your son figure it out for himself and a father doing it all for him. That's how it was when I was a kid too. My dad insisted that I lead the project. He helped me do whatever I wanted done, but he wanted me to be in charge, which was fine while we were making the car, but sad in the race because I always got beat by some kid whose engineer dad had done the whole thing for him.

Looking back, I can see that maybe that boy won the Pinewood Derby because of his dad's help, but where does it stop? And at some point, it must, because to become an adult, we all must step out on our own.

The disciples knew about that.

"Now after John was arrested, Jesus came to Galilee, proclaiming the good news of God... And as he passed along the Sea of Galilee, there were two brothers who were mending nets with their father. Immediately he called them and they left their father Zebedee in the boat with the hired men and followed him."

What about that?

You've heard a story like that before. Dad's an optometrist. He builds up his own office, and it's not easy making it on his own, what with Lens Crafters and Wal-Mart basically giving glasses away. But he keeps going because he has a daughter who's a student at the School of Optometry and Vision Science, and he dreams of handing that practice over to her. Only guess what? She falls in love with some guy and they start a family.

What about that?

Or consider this father. Last summer I bought this pasta maker at a yard sale. I bought it for 20 bucks, which is a lot to spend at a yard sale, but I handed it over because I thought: "What a great bonding experience this will be for me and our girls. Who cares that you can just buy a box of spaghetti for 99 cents – they'll love it." And I guess they did, or Lily did for about 5 minutes, so mostly it was I making pasta, then cleaning it up for probably two hours. It got all stuck together, so it wasn't all that pretty, but it tasted good – and the receipt was still in there. New, that thing cost $175, which I would have paid because I love spending time with our girls, but they don't always want to do what I want them to do.

You know what I'm talking about?

Father Zebedee would understand. You think old father Zebedee didn't love having his sons out there with him? You think he didn't have dreams like that optometrist? And now to whom is he going to pass those nets down? One of the hired hands who is only after a day's pay? He can't do that. What is he going to do?

A hard thing about being a parent is that you can't help but build expectations that you have no control over – and a hard thing about being a child is that you can't help but disappoint your parents even though half the time you don't even know why.

But eventually every mother realizes that her sons have to decide on their own, every father realizes that he can't stand in the way of his daughter's dreams, and every child who successfully grows into adulthood has realized that he has to make his own Pinewood Derby car, and even if it loses every race, at least he tried and did it on his own.

Faith is like that too.

Last Monday was Dr. Martin Luther King Jr. Day, and once in a sermon, he shared a story of such an experience. For him it wasn't a Pinewood Derby car that he had to build on his own, but it was about a long night in Birmingham, Alabama where he needed God, and he had to turn to God on his own.

Early in the day, his life and the lives of his wife and children were threatened because the words that he spoke and the changes that he supported inspired someone to throw a brick through his window with a note attached.

The note told him that if he didn't stop talking and get out of town, his life and the lives of his wife and children would be in jeopardy. Dr. King wanted nothing more than to have his father by his side so that he could comfort him, so that together they might turn to God in prayer. But, his father was about 150 miles away.

That night, Dr. King got up and made a pot of coffee because he couldn't sleep. He pondered the brick that had been thrown through the window of the house his wife and children were sleeping in and he began to pray, praying for what he said may have been the first time he had ever really prayed in his life. "My father wasn't there to do it for me," he said, "So I prayed to God myself."

All believers must do that.

There's an old saying that goes: "The Lord doesn't have any grandchildren." What that means is that developing a relationship with God isn't something that parents can do for their children – to God, being related to a Christian isn't the same as being one yourself. We all must learn what it means to be the children of God on our own.

At some point, we must all learn to follow Christ by ourselves. Even if we've been dragged into a church like this one for our entire childhood, at some point we must get up and go ourselves. We must make the choice, and for some of us that means not just doing it on our own without our parents, but following Christ despite them.

Somebody asked me the other day if my parents were excited when I told them I felt called to the ministry. My parents knew far too much about the lifestyle that serving God as a pastor requires, to be excited. They were worried. And still, they talk to us about going up to their house for Christmas, refusing to accept the reality that I'll be preaching every Christmas Eve from now until I retire.

But that's nothing really. Consider this daughter. She's the first one in her family to go to college. Some parents would be proud, but hers can't understand and don't see the point. "Come back and mend the nets," she can hear them say.

Every church officer who was just ordained and installed probably faced some version of that. A call came from the Officer Nominating Committee asking them to serve this church in a leadership role, and if not in their ear then surely in their head were the voices of spouses telling them, "But we have kids to raise and a house to run. Don't say yes. Come back and mend the nets." Friends may have said, "Someone else will say yes. It doesn't have to be you. Come back and mend the nets."

This is life.

I was in Confirmation Class years ago, but my friends got the bright idea to skip class and hang out behind the Cotton Building. That was fun for a while, but at some point, I started feeling guilty and was easing my way back to where I was supposed to be. "Come back here and mend the nets," my friends called – and I told them, "I'll be right back, I just need to use the bathroom." I wasn't strong enough to tell them I wanted to go back to class. If I said that I was leaving them to go to class, would they still be my friends?

It costs something, doesn't it?

And parents, we raise these children the best we can – then we must let them go, and that may mean they move far away, destroying all of our plans and expectations -- even breaking our hearts.

But who can blame them?

For when the chance for new life comes walking down the beach, calling us to follow, we all must listen.

Amen.

Part 6

From Transfiguration Sunday to Easter

The account of Christ appearing on the mountaintop, accompanied by Moses and Elijah, is extraordinary and it leads us to face the reality of Christ's trajectory towards His own death. From Transfiguration Sunday we are led into the season of Lent, and then finally to His victorious resurrection.

Down from the Mountain
2 Kings 2:1-12 and Mark 9:2-9

As I'm sure you've noticed by now, in addition to being Transfiguration Sunday, today is Scout Sunday. Some of the scouts who meet here at our church began the service by bringing in the flags, and I am thankful to serve a church where Boy and Girl Scouts are invited to meet, and where the Cub Scouts have their Pinewood Derby. It's wonderful.

As I've mentioned before, I was once a Cub Scout. Carl Dimare was my den leader. A few months ago, he gave me a picture of our den that he took during a camp-out at the Woodruff Scout Camp. It's on my desk. Den 11. My Dad and I are standing right next to each other, and now I look more like him than the 8-year-old version of me.

Participation in scouts was a family tradition of ours. Both my Dad and my younger brother are Eagle Scouts. When they were active here in Troop 252 my brother and several others who are members here today were signed up and ready to go on a big canoe trip up to the Boundary Waters. Those are the lakes that dot the border between Minnesota and Canada. When my Dad couldn't go, I was invited to go in his place.

This was a big deal for me. I was excited to go, but you know, the whole ride up there I'm starting to worry. I remember getting nervous about what life in the great outdoors was going to be like for a full 10-day span. And then they showed us what we were going to be eating and I got really nervous.

But here's the thing about camping. Here's the thing about big trips in the great outdoors. It takes a little while to get used to it. You must ease into a trip like that one. But once you're into it, day two or three, you start to forget that civilization even exists, and you say to yourself as you're watching the sun set, "I could just stay right out here for a while."

I could just paddle this canoe with my brother, Hal McClain, and all the others. Live on MRE's and Tang. We'll be just fine. I remember thinking that about day 3 or 4 of that trip watching the sun set. It seems like you hardly ever take the time to watch the sun set until you're camping, and as I did, I felt like making a life for myself out there in the woods.

Do you know that feeling?

Not everyone does. Andrew McIntosh, our Youth Director, nuanced Henry David Thoreau this week. He said, "I went to the woods to live deliberately,

161

and I deliberately went right back home to civilization." But if you know the feeling that I'm talking about then you can start to imagine what is going on in Peter's head, because just as it can be nice to be on a long canoe trip or to spend a week on the beach and away from it all, you can't stay up on top of a mountain.

But Peter was ready to stay.

I love this about Peter.

Of course, everybody loves Peter, because Peter says the dumb thing that everyone else is thinking.

"Rabbi, it is good for us to be here; let us make three dwellings, one for you, one for Moses, and one for Elijah."

Isn't that surely what they were all thinking?

There they were, up on top of this mountain. At the top they see their teacher, their friend, transfigured before them, and his clothes became dazzling white. There appeared to them Elijah, the Great Prophet, with Moses who led the people out of slavery in Egypt. These heroes of the faith were talking to their Jesus, so of course, why not pitch a tent and stay there for a while?

You know what I'm talking about.

You have an amazing experience. You escape from the world for a little while and your spirit lifts.

The Youth Group goes to Montreat, North Carolina for the big youth conference. It's a week full of these great worship services. Everyone meets in small groups composed of youth from all over that start to feel like family. Then you go hike to the top of Lookout Mountain and somebody says, "I wish we could just stay here forever."

Of course, you do.

But you can't.

Why?

Because real life isn't lived up on a mountain.

You must come down from the mountain to really live.

Let me tell you what I mean.

Back in Columbia, Tennessee, the night after Dylan Roof walked into Emmanuel African Methodist Episcopal Church for a Bible study in Charleston, then walked out a murderer, the pastors of the AME churches in Columbia called on every pastor and every elected official to meet for a worship service at St. Paul African Methodist Episcopal Church.

It started about 7:00 in the evening.

There were a lot of people there.

I remember preaching, then going back to my pew to sing with everyone else. We sang one hymn, then another, and it was so hot that I felt like I was sweating through my suit jacket, but the Holy Spirit was in that place and everyone there could feel it.

A few more pastors went to preach. Then a man named Chris Poynter went to the pulpit. He was the Executive Director of the Boys and Girls Club and he told us that this worship service was a joyous event, that he hadn't felt so inspired since the pep rallies back in High School. "But the game is tomorrow," he said. "It's not tonight that is going to change our community or our world; it's what we do tomorrow when we go back to the real world. How will we live then?"

You see, you can't stay on the canoe trip.

You can't just have a wonderful worship service and think that the daemon of racism is dead and gone.

You must come down from the mountain and back to the real world, because it's in the valley that life is lived.

So, Peter can't make three dwellings.

They can't just stay up there.

No, they had to go down the mountain, and as they were coming down the mountain, Jesus ordered them to tell no one about what they had seen until after the Son of Man had risen from the dead.

Now this isn't the first time Jesus told them that he would die. In fact, Jesus had been telling them about how he would have to undergo great suffering and be rejected by the elders, the chief priests, and the scribes. He had even told them that he would be killed, and after three days rise again, but I bet you that this is the first time they believed him, because it's one thing for your friend to mention something of that gravity in conversation and it's another thing to see your friend transfigured before your eyes as he talks with Elijah and Moses.

I believe the real reason Peter wanted to stay up on that mountain is because Peter now knew, as Elisha the Prophet knew, that he would soon lose his friend whom he loved. Peter knew Jesus would go down that mountain and if he kept preaching and healing the way he had been preaching and healing, then he would be on his way to the Cross.

You know this scared Peter, so he wanted to stay up on that mountain, and you know that's what Peter wanted because that's what we all want:

To avoid the pain … to reduce the risk … to never lose the people we love. But Jesus knew that you can't live life on the mountain.

Life is lived down in the valley, and so He goes down, because you can't be the Savior of the World if you're hiding from the world.

You can't be the King of Kings if you never face your people.

You can't live your life's purpose if you're afraid to live.

Life is lived in the valley, and so we must take those mountaintop experiences, those lessons that we learn from the woods, and we take all that back to our life in the valley because if we don't, then we can't be a blessing to the world.

And maybe it's hard. Risky.

It's like the difference between singing in the shower and singing in front of people like all these good choir members do week after week. Or how well I preach my sermons when I'm practicing in my office. I have this lectern set up in front of a mirror, and man – you should hear me preach when there's no one there to listen.

That's because everything is easier if it doesn't count. But if you want to make an impact on this world, if you want to live out your purpose on this earth, if you have a gift that you just must share, then you have to come down from the mountain top to sing your song in the valley.

That's life.

So, that's what Jesus did.

And that is what leads to His death.

This reality is sobering, isn't it? And as it was true for Him, so it's true for us. You can't just stay up on the mountaintop. You can't live out in the woods any more than your four years of college should stretch out into 5 or 6. The point is to prepare you for life in the real world, not to avoid it. But the real world can kill you.

You know what I'm talking about.

Valentine's Day is this week. Wednesday. And Valentine's Day is risky. Say you pine for some young lady or young man. You dream about him or you imagine the day when she'll finally notice you, but do you say anything? No – if you say something, she might reject you. But if you don't try, you never know.

The same is true of writing. Who knows how many great writers out there have yet to sit down and write a book? Who knows how many people have a story to tell but are afraid to tell it? That's because writing hurts. Many writers have offered some version of the great quote: "Writing is easy, you just open a vein and bleed." Which is to say that you can't do it if you are unwilling to come down from the mountain. That's a place where life is all possibility. Up on the mountain no one has to get hurt. But to write you must go down to the place where rejection and pain are both possible – the valley is where life is lived.

Life is lived in the valley – where there is risk.

I learned earlier this week that just before Dr. Martin Luther King Jr. gave his "I Have a Dream" speech, a white Presbyterian, Rev. Eugene Carson Blake spoke. He told the crowd assembled, "We Presbyterians have come to this Civil Rights Movement late, but we are here." Why were we late?

Because walking into the valley, stepping away from what is and stepping towards what could be, challenging the status quo, worrying our parents, speaking out on difficult issues – all of that is a risk that few people take because most of us are just fine with building our tents up on the mountain top.

But you know what Dr. King said? Not so long after he spoke in Washington DC with Rev. Blake, he said, "Longevity has its place. But I'm not concerned about that now. I just want to do God's will."

We Christians - we can't just be "Mountain Top Christians".

We can't just be Sunday Morning Christians.

We must take the lessons that we learn here, the feelings that fill our souls here, the new life that we hope for here and walk down the mountain side, out onto Kennesaw Avenue and Church Street and to our work place and our neighborhoods so that the Gospel of Jesus Christ will be proclaimed.

And yes, there's a risk …

For when it comes to what matters, there is always risk.

Then the question becomes, would you rather just play at being a Christian, or are you ready to follow Him where He leads?

Amen.

Be Reconciled
2 Corinthians 5:20b – 6:2

Ash Wednesday is a relatively new concept for Presbyterians.

Of course, it's not new at all. It's ancient. But it occurs to me that Ash Wednesday still warrants an explanation. After this service, if you go to Kroger, someone may ask you about the smear on your forehead, and I want you to have a good answer.

The Ash Wednesday ashes could be explained this way:

The grass-plot before the jail, in Prison Lane, on a certain summer morning, not less than two centuries ago, was occupied by a pretty large number of the inhabitants of Boston, all with their eyes intently fastened on the iron-clamped oaken door…

These inhabitants, both men and women, busied themselves debating what should become of the woman who was to be released.

This woman has brought shame upon us all, and ought to die, one shouted, but then the lock of the prison-door turned, and out came the condemned, Mistress Hester Prynne.

She bore in her arms a child, a baby of some three months, who winked and turned aside its little face from the too vivid light of day, having grown accustomed to the grey twilight of a dungeon.

When the young woman – the mother of the child – stood fully revealed before the crowd, it seemed to be her first impulse to clasp the infant closely to her, not so much by an impulse of motherly affection as that she might thereby conceal a certain token, which was wrought or fastened into her dress. [For] on the breast of her gown appeared the letter A.

Every English teacher knows that these words open *The Scarlet Letter* by Nathaniel Hawthorn, and tells the story of a woman whose guilt was broadcast by the letter A embroidered on all her clothes.

There, for everyone to see, was the sign of her sin.

What then is this ash that we will soon have on our foreheads?

It is our own scarlet letter – it is the symbol of our guilt, our sin, our mistakes, our failures.

But here's the miraculous thing about Ash Wednesday – the miracle for this church and all those like it – we all wear our mark boldly, willingly for everyone at Kroger to see.

My ashes will be the sign that I am guilty.

Guilty by what I have said and by what I have left unsaid.

Guilty by what I have done and by what I have left undone.

Guilty, disobedient, prideful, selfish, distracted, judgmental, and just as deserving of punishment as every other Puritan assembled outside that prison door.

Now consider that. Imagine if everyone who was guilty had a letter on his or her chest. That's Ash Wednesday.

And, when everyone wears his or her scarlet letter, the symbol's power changes.

In here, all of us, with our shame, broadcast for all to see. It's not like the Puritan Settlement, the Middle School, or any other place where the ones who pretend to be innocent circle around the guilty like vultures, because in here we are all acknowledging the truth of who we are. Not one of us has the right to cast the first stone.

These ashes help us to get the truth - what we know about ourselves deep down - out in the open. The shame that lurks in here comes out, and once the truth is out, we can stop pretending; we can stop fearing, and shame loses its power when it's not kept a secret. Then, we are all finally free to follow this great charge that Paul gives in 2 Corinthians: "Be reconciled," he says.

And "be reconciled" is so different from "be condemned" or "feel guilty" or "you should be ashamed of yourself," because this charge from the Apostle Paul gets to the heart of what our God wants – for our God wants reconciliation.

Not condemnation – reconciliation.

Not shame – redemption.

Not secrets – but open hearts.

Tonight is about acknowledging sin, but it isn't about guilt.

168

This isn't about shame.

This service and these ashes are about confessing our stumbling blocks and putting back together our relationship with God that's been harmed by our human actions - our finally being real.

Hiding our problems won't make them go away — so we wear this sign on our foreheads and say it plain: "I am a sinner, in need of forgiveness, and I'm ready today to accept the grace our God provides."

Why wait?

Why hide in the darkness any longer, when we can come into the light right now? That's what tonight is about.

We read in 2 Corinthians: "See, now is the acceptable time; see, now is the day of salvation!"

These ashes are my confession that I have not been who I ought to have been, but I am ready to be made new. So, this Lent I will give up what stands in my way.

Maybe I will give up Facebook. Then I will spend no more of my precious time searching for political comments that only fuel my anger, and further wedge the divide between my relatives and me.

Why give up chocolate when I could give up the bad habit that keeps me from reconciliation?

If politics is dividing you and your sister — give up the news for these 40 Days of Lent. The world will still turn without your watching, but that chasm between you and her will only grow unless you change the conversation.

Let us give up building up walls for Lent. Spend this time that we have building bridges.

Can we give up fear — anxiety — perfectionism, to really live the life that honors our Father in Heaven?

Be reconciled to God.

Give up what holds you back and divides you from the one sitting next to you — give up what keeps you from listening to the Good News and what distracts you from the Holy Spirit. Take out those earbuds and turn off the TV long enough to enjoy the world God created for you to enjoy.

And if you do – your relationship with your Creator will be strengthened – and you will give God what God wants – not shame, but reconciliation.

Be reconciled to God.

Open wide your heart – for in the Lord Jesus Christ, who suffered for 40 days in the desert only to face a brutal death on the Cross, is the obvious sign that God's heart is open wide to you.

Remove the stumbling blocks.

Tear down the walls.

Turn off the phones.

Accept the grace and let it flow out of you. Be reconciled!

Amen.

Divine Things and Human Things
Genesis 17:1-7 and 15-16, Mark 8:31-38

I watched the *Emoji Movie* this last week.

If you're a parent then you might be thinking, "What he means is that his kids watched the Emoji Movie while he looked at his phone or read a book or something." But that's not what I mean. What I mean is that I watched the Emoji Movie. One top critic reviewed this movie and wrote: "The film is boldly bad, yes, but also boldly boring." Another wrote: "Disregard that PG rating and keep your children far away from director Tony Leondis' vile animated faux-comedy." These are harsh words, and some would heed such warnings, but not I. No, after watching the first half of the movie with our daughters, I had to tear myself away to get dressed and get to the church last Tuesday morning, so I watched the second half by myself Wednesday because I had a vested interested in finding out how the movie would end.

Why? Why would I care so much about a frowny face character that doesn't just want to frown? (He also wants to laugh and cry.) ... Because for some reason I could relate to him.

I also started to care about the other main character. Princess Emoji ran away because she wanted to be an outlaw computer hacker emoji. Now granted, none of this describes what anyone would call a good movie, but I have a feeling that every person in this room, whether she knows what an emoji is or not, has felt the pressure to be not what she was created to be but who everyone told her that she was supposed to be.

I'm working on that too.

All the critics told me I would hate this movie, but I kinda loved it, and that's what I want to preach about this morning. We live in a country where everyone is telling us what to think. And not just about movies.

Even Russia is trying to tell us what to think, how to vote, and what to feel about our neighbors and our political candidates, and if we can't learn to think for ourselves, then there goes our democracy, our freedom, and our faith.

There is a very real struggle at work in our world today, as forces fight for control of our human hearts which must determine whether we will be ourselves or we will lose ourselves to the pressures of conformity.

To spoil the Emoji Movie, I'll tell you that despite social pressure, Frowny Face gained the courage to cry and laugh out in public, and Princess got to be an outlaw, because not every girl wants to be a princess, and in the end, the world changed and everything turned out perfectly. I suppose that's the happy ending we are all after, but getting there is a struggle.

You heard what happened with Jesus.

Last Sunday Rev. Joe Brice preached a beautiful sermon concerning Jesus's temptation in the wilderness. But the temptation didn't end there. After 40 days in the desert with the devil tempting him to take power and seize control, to be someone other than who He knew in His heart He was meant to be, Jesus emerged from the desert only to be tempted by His friend. We read from the Gospel of Mark:

Then he began to teach them that the Son of Man must undergo great suffering, and be rejected by the elders, the chief priests, and the scribes, and be killed, and after three days rise again. He said all of this quite openly. And Peter took him aside and began to rebuke him.

Why? Because Peter didn't want Jesus to be that kind of messiah.

Peter didn't want Jesus to upset all of those people.

Peter wanted a nice, quiet messiah ... one who would be everyone's hero and who would one day retire with him to the beach, and together Peter and Jesus could look back on all their years of ministry and Peter would say to his friend in the beach chair next to him, "Jesus, it's been a wonderful life, hasn't it?"

Maybe there was a part of Jesus that wanted this kind of life too, but He must rebuke Peter just as He rebuked the devil back in the wilderness: "Get behind me, Satan!" He said to His friend. "For you are setting your mind not on divine things but on human things."

Isn't it easy to set your mind on human things?

The great Rev. Billy Graham died this week. One of his most famous quotes is: "My home is in heaven. I'm just passing through this world." But it's easy to get stuck in this world.

Isn't it easy to set your mind on human things?

A Puritan prayer book that I love says it this way: "O Savior of Sinners, raise me above the smiles and frowns of the world, regarding it as a light thing to be judged by humans."

Do you know anyone who needs to pray that prayer?

I know I need it. Maybe you do too.

And Poor Marco Rubio needs a prayer like that one.

Did you see him? I was hurting for Senator Rubio this week. It seems like he gets enough abuse with the President calling him Little Marco, but it got worse. On Wednesday, a student from Marjory Stoneman Douglas High School in Florida asked him if he'd stop accepting money from the NRA, and poor Senator Rubio ... you don't need to have seen the video to imagine the face he was making, because he was making that face that we all know when we feel so trapped that we can't win for losing.

We ask ourselves: "How will I even open my mouth, when I'm faced with mollifying one group of people but disappointing another?"

"How can I speak, when someone out there is about to walk out of this place and hate me forever based on how I answer?"

You know this struggle. It's a fool's errand but I've been that fool again and again and again, and I bet you have too.

You lean one way and you're someone's hero, but someone else's enemy. It sure does feel like you're dying a slow death if you are unable to rise above the smiles and frowns of the world. It's impossible for you to regard it as a light thing to be judged by humans, because your mind is set on human things.

Jesus said to Peter: "You are setting your mind not on divine things but on human things," and if that's the way we choose to live, then it's going to be nothing but torture from here on out.

It was that way for me in my first year of ministry. I began my ministry at Good Shepherd Presbyterian Church out in Lilburn, Georgia, and I was going to be everything to everybody even if it killed me.

Someone asked me if I liked to listen to the Fish – that Christian radio station -- and so I started to listen to it. A group wanted to start a Bible study, and so I helped them get it going. Then another group wanted one, then another, and before long I was leading a Bible study every day of the week, listening to the Fish in the car, and there was no place of solace.

Basically, the hardest thing about my first year of ministry was that I was trying to be not the pastor who I was, but the pastor who I thought members wanted me to be.

One morning I woke up with a rash on my stomach. It started out red and itchy, and it wouldn't go away. Sara finally sent me to the doctor. He told me that is was hives, and that he could give me some medicine for it, but really it was just from stress. What I really needed to do was find a way to relax.

"You're a preacher, right?" my doctor asked.

I told him that I was, and so he said again, "What you need to do is find a way to relax. Have you ever heard of prayer?"

What is prayer, but the constant reminder that our identity comes not from humans but from God ... that our primary relationship must be between our Creator and us? To quote that great prayer for illumination: "Lord, among all the changing words of this generation, speak to us your eternal Word which does not change," because it is God's voice that must define us rather than the whispers of the gossips or the pressure of the lobbyist.

"Who do they say that I am?" Jesus asked his disciples. And the difference between His asking this question and our asking the same of ourselves is that He didn't really care who anybody said He was. He already knew.

But what about Senator Rubio?

If your actions are tied to public opinion or interest group donations, can you really be free?

And what about the accused shooter, Nikolas Cruz?

If you must murder the people who hurt your feelings, if you aren't man enough to voice your anger, then you are letting your out-of-control emotions and other people define who you are.

We all must slow down and think.

Or better yet – we all must slow down and listen – because in our baptism the Lord already told us who we are: "You are mine, my beloved, and with you I am well pleased." The difference between all of us and Jesus is that He never forgot it. He was always bold to believe it. And He never depended on humans to tell Him who He was or how He should live.

Let our prayer be: "O Savior of Sinners, raise me above the smiles and frowns of the world, regarding it as a light thing to be judged by humans."

And may our song be like the hymn we sang at the 8:30 service:

But if, forgetful, we should find your yoke is hard to bear;
If worldly pressures fray the mind and love itself cannot unwind
Its tangled skein of care; our inward life repair.[7]

For how will we make it to the Kingdom of Heaven, if we long for the approval of this broken world?

We must set our minds not on human things, but on divine things.

Amen.

---

[7] Fred Pratt Green, *How Clear is Our Vocation Lord,* 1981.

Braid the Whip
Malachi 3:1-7 and John 2:13-22

You might know that last summer our youth group went on a mission trip to Mexico. This was the first trip back there after several years of not going, and when Erroll Eckford, the chair of the Family Council, reported at our congregational meeting that our youth group built two houses in Mexico, it took me right back to the trips I went on to Mexico as a high school student.

These were life-changing trips for me, and they continue to be for those who go. But kids are kids, and discipline was an issue back when I was in high school, which makes sense. How do you keep a large group of high school students under control when driving them across the country? Some would say, "Well, you don't." But our leaders tried to keep us in line, and one technique that I remembered during Erroll's report last Wednesday night were these bracelets our leaders gave us when I was a sophomore or junior in high school. It was just a simple bracelet that we all wore, but on it were the letters, WWJD, which stood for, "What would Jesus do?"

Maybe you remember these bracelets. I imagine that we were given them so that before we did something against the rules, like sneak out of our hotel rooms after dark, we'd ask ourselves, "Now, is this something that Jesus would do?"

The bracelets made us stop and think: "Would Jesus make fun of his friend?"

Or, "Would Jesus conceal Ex-Lax in a chocolate wrapper and trick his friend into eating it?"

We did that anyway, but Jesus wouldn't have. No, Jesus would be nice. "Jesus was always nice" is what we were thinking as we wore these bracelets.

But Jesus wasn't always nice.

I'm not saying that He was ever mean. I don't believe that, but from Scripture you can see that Jesus wasn't just nice, or peaceful, or serene.

Last Friday I took our girls to tour the childhood home of Dr. Martin Luther King Jr. When looking into the dining room, our tour guide told us that Dr. King's father required all the children to quote a verse of Scripture before taking their first bite of supper, and young Martin was prone to quote John 11:35, "Jesus wept," the shortest verse in the entire Bible.

That verse, "Jesus wept," and another like it, "Jesus laughed," are short, but they tell us so much about this Savior of ours whose emotional life we are prone to reduce to a perpetually Heavenly gaze. We think of that painting of Jesus by Warner Sallman. He's bearded, and looking off in the distance, neither stoic nor emotional, but just serene.

Then there's the other popular image of Jesus welcoming the little children, which of course He did. But He wasn't just nice. He also wept, He also laughed, and He also got angry.

He had emotions, just like we do.

He was sometimes sad, just as we are.

He often laughed, just like we do.

And He sometimes got angry, just like we do. But the difference between Him and us is in how He expressed his emotions.

That's something we don't all know how to do, even though Mr. Rogers tried to teach us.

I saw a video this week where Mr. Rogers walks towards the camera and he says, "I'm angry."

Of course, he doesn't look angry. It's hard to look angry in a cardigan. Then he starts singing,

What do you do with the mad that you feel,

When you feel so mad you could bite.

When the whole wide world seems Oh, so wrong,

And nothing you do seems very right.

That's life, isn't it? We get mad, but what do we do with the mad that we feel?

Mr. Rogers has this other song where he plays the piano because he's angry, and he sings this very un-angry sounding song. "I'm angry. I'm angry." He doesn't sound very angry singing this. It's hard to sound angry when you sing, but then he sings, "I'm angry. I'm angry. And I can tell you why."

We read from the Gospel of John that Jesus told those who were selling the doves, "Take these things out of here! Stop making my Father's house a marketplace!"

That's one way that Jesus's anger is different from so much of ours.

He feels the feeling that we feel, but He can say what He's angry about.

Not everyone I know can do that.

In fact, I know a whole lot of people who won't even admit that they're angry. I'm one of them.

It's hard for me to say that I'm angry, because I think I'm always supposed to be nice.

My parents would ask me, "Joe, what's wrong?"

I'd tell them, "Nothing."

These days, Sara will ask me, "What are you so mad about?"

And I'll say, "I'm mad about your always asking me if I'm mad."

That's not true of course, but that's what I say, because just that simple thing: saying what I'm angry about is hard for me to do. And I'm not alone; so let me say that in taking a lesson from Jesus, we first must accept the reality that being angry is a part of being human. Then we must come to terms with the truth that sometimes our anger is telling us something so important that we can't ignore it. We must say something, and maybe even do something.

Let's use the Son of God as our example: What was Jesus angry about? His Father's house had been turned into a marketplace. You can understand why He'd be upset about that. Anger isn't always so unreasonable. Most of the time we are justified in our anger, but we get all messed up in coming to terms with what it is that we're angry about, and then deciding what it is that we're going to do about it.

The most wonderful detail in our Gospel lesson for today is there in verse 15, and we read: "Making a whip of cords, he drove all of them out of the temple, both the sheep and the cattle." In all four of the Gospel accounts of Jesus's life and ministry, He storms into the Temple, kicking over tables, scattering the coins of the money changers, and setting free the animals, but only in John does He first make a whip of cords.

Do you know how long it takes to braid a whip of cords?

I don't. And I don't know not only because I've never done it, but also because when I get angry, I don't stop to do anything that might help me calm down or process my thoughts. Instead, I either just start talking without thinking or go silent and brooding. Hardly, if ever, do I stop what I'm doing to sit down to think about why it is that I'm angry and what it is that I'm going to do about it.

Jesus is different. Jesus gets angry and then He braids a whip of cords. Do you know how counter cultural that is?

There are those among us who get angry and send off a Twitter message.

Others get angry, then yell at the first person they see.

There's an old cartoon I remember where the boss yells at Dad in the office. Then Dad comes home and yells at Mom in the kitchen. Mom goes upstairs to yell at their son, who then walks out into the yard to kick the dog.

Anger. It can destroy a family like a disease that gets passed on from one to the next.

Another thing we may do with anger is keep it inside so that it rots our guts and hollows our spirit. Some try to drown it with liquor, numb it with drugs, either of which is destructive. Few take the time to sit down and really think about it. "What am I mad about?" Then, "what am I going to do about it?"

The knee jerk response to get somebody fired or lock somebody up can do more harm than good,

We must braid the whip, because in our world today we are all angry about something. We must stop and listen to our anger for it to do us or our world any good. If you read the article this morning covering Chief Justice Harris Hines's farewell address to the judiciary as he prepares for retirement, then you know that he has worked to fight the old "lock him up" order from the bench, to get to a better solution.

As a culture, as a nation, we must learn what to do with anger, because right now anger is tearing us apart. But do you know what it's supposed to do?

Purify us.

Significant background for understanding what it means for Jesus to storm the Temple is found in the Old Testament book of Malachi. Do you ever read Malachi? I'll give two free tickets to the Talent Show to anyone who can turn to Malachi. Just kidding. But let me remind you of what we read earlier: "The Lord whom you seek will suddenly come to His Temple." And when He gets there, He won't just be nice, walking around shaking hands and kissing babies. No. According to the Prophet Malachi, "He is like a refiner's fire and like Fuller's soap. He will purify the descendants of Levi and refine them like gold and silver, until they present offerings to the Lord in righteousness."

Jesus, fueled by anger, purifies the Temple so that it might no longer be a marketplace, but a Temple.

No longer a den of thieves, but a sanctuary for the hurting.

No longer a place where money is exchanged and debts are paid, but a place where debts are forgiven – and how did He do it? Through anger. Through an anger that is frustrated with what is and directed towards that which stands in the way of a better future.

Jesus didn't get upset at the Temple only to go home and type a rant on Facebook.

He didn't go home to pout to His mama.

Nor did He walk into the Temple with an AR-15.

Instead, He braids a whip.

And after braiding it He kicked over tables, He scattered money, He chased off livestock, and no one got hurt. No one died. And through Him and the Temple that was His body, we are given a new relationship with God and an entrance into the Kingdom of Heaven. From Him we must learn to braid the whip.

For in your frustration with this world lies the motivation to make some changes.

Braid the whip.

Because you deserve better, and your anger, channeled, will help you get there.

Braid the whip.

Stop and listen, for the Spirit still speaks, calling us away from the ways of death that we have grown used to, and towards new life.

Amen.

Come to the Light
Numbers 21:4-9 and John 3:1-21

As I said last Sunday, the Gospel of John is full of important details, and some of those details are both significant and unique to John's Gospel. The important detail John gives us at the beginning of our second Scripture lesson for today is this detail that a Pharisee named Nicodemus, a leader of the Jews…came to Jesus by night.

Not in the day – by night.

And you know why people choose to do some things at night.

No one should buy a new car under the cover of darkness. No one sneaks in to a Post Office to deliver mail after the sun has set. This Pharisee, Nicodemus, goes to see Jesus, not when people would have been out and noticing things, but at night when the Mrs. Kravitzes of the world were in bed sleeping. Why then does he go at night?

You have that think that Nicodemus goes to see Jesus at night because he doesn't want anyone to see him going over there.

He's like the guy you know who parks at the Publix but goes into the liquor store.

You know this kind of person.

He's like the woman whose husband is drawing unemployment, but she maxes out the credit cards on a big vacation so she can still send out a Christmas card of her family at the beach.

Why?

Because all of us are interested in keeping up appearances and so often that's doing us more harm than good.

Nicodemus's going to see Jesus at night reminds me of Jan Brady when she hid her glasses in her purse so Bernie McGuire wouldn't know that she wears them. Maybe you remember that episode of the Brady Bunch. Jan rode home from the library with her glasses still in her purse and crashes into the garage.

Isn't it strange that sometimes we'd choose wreaking our bicycles over being seen for who we really are?

Nicodemus goes to see Jesus at night, and you know why? Because we all go to Jesus out of our own version of the night, not sure whether we're ready to be really seen. We are not sure if we want anyone to know who we really are and what we're struggling with. Most of us feel this so profoundly that we even hide the truth from our doctors, our children, and some even feel compelled to hide it here at church.

We cover up our struggles with Easter Bonnets.

It's hard to ask the Sunday School class to pray for you when you're struggling, because we'd all rather brag to them about how well our kids are doing or how we're going to redecorate our kitchen.

Everyone is glad to come to church when preparing for a wedding day -- meeting with the organist, picking out the flowers, talking about the details, and going in to the pastor's office to discuss the ceremony. But it's so much harder to get here when we're going through a divorce, even though that's exactly what this place is for.

This is a hospital.

We come here because we're sick and want to be healed, but it's so hard to come to terms with our own affliction. We'd all prefer to be well, so that's what we pretend, and that's the story that we tell ourselves and our friends.

Nicodemus is afraid to go see Jesus in the light of day for the same reason that people use Facebook as a giant forum for pretending that everything is OK.

We must, however, be real to someone. If we don't, hiding the truth will kill us. But telling the truth can require overcoming some serious obstacles.

In the words of John Calvin, that great theologian who laid the groundwork of our Presbyterian faith: "Nicodemus was of the Pharisees, and this designation was no doubt regarded by his countrymen as honorable. Hence, we are reminded that they who occupy a lofty station in the world are for the most part entangled by very dangerous snares."

And what are those snares?

The snares of decorum that keep people from being honest.

The snares of familial obligation that push some to uphold a certain image and keep them from airing their dirty laundry.

The snares of appearances that keep the powerful from apology and any semblance of weakness.

The snares of ego-driven fear that keep the religious from enjoying the benefits of grace, for sometimes even we Presbyterians choose to appear like we have it all together rather than reveal our need for mercy.

Nicodemus goes to Jesus at night because he is one who feels inclined to maintain an air of having things under control. He is challenged by words like: "I don't know what to do" or better yet, words like: "I'm lost and need help." They are so hard to say that only the bravest among us can just come right out and say them.

By so many these words are mostly whispered, and only then if no one is looking.

Maybe while in the car, when the one talking and the one listening are both looking at the road and don't have to face each other.

Nicodemus goes to Jesus at night because how else could he say, "Rabbi, we know that you are a teacher who has come from God; for no one can do these signs that you do apart from the presence of God."

Think about those words.

"Rabbi", which means teacher, says a Pharisee named Nicodemus, a leader of the Jews, who is supposed to be a teacher himself.

Then, "We know that you are a teacher who has come from God; for no one can do these signs that you do apart from the presence of God."

What a confession this is! And I say that it is a confession, an act full of precious vulnerability, because Nicodemus had all the credentials, all the certifications. He was by all standards a holy man of Israel, and yet this Jesus of Nazareth is the one who is doing all the signs and wonders.

You know what this is like? It's like an orthopedic surgeon going to a chiropractor.

Seeking out help from him requires complete vulnerability.

For fear of being attacked, some never let their guard down this much.

Show weakness – never.

Admit that someone else can do it better – no way.

Ask for directions? I'd rather drive all night having no idea where I'm going than risk being shamed by a gas station attendant who'd look down on me saying: "You're not from around here, are you?"

Vulnerability – even small acts of vulnerability are tough.

Someone asks how you're doing. "I'm fine. I'm fine," and I'll go on pretending that I am because taking the risk of being honest is just too painful a thought.

And why is that? Many experts believe it is due to the power of shame.

In his book, *Spirituality in Recovery, a 12 Step Approach,* Dr. John Ishee, a good Presbyterian and the retired Director of Pastoral Care at Cumberland Heights Alcohol and Drug Treatment Center in Nashville writes:

There is an important difference between guilt and shame. Guilt is the feeling that we have done something wrong – that we have violated our conscience. Shame is more. It is the feeling that we are wrong – flawed, defective, less than unworthy, deficient, disgraceful, bad – even evil. Guilt prompts us to think or say I made a mistake. Shame prompts us to think or say I am a mistake.

There are religious groups and churches at work in this world who are so capable of inspiring their congregations to feel shame that they will convince you that it's not a matter of whether you're going to Hell, but just how soon. For years, I believed, and some days I still do, that sin is not so much a reality that can be forgiven as a state that I am sentenced to permanently. "Sinner!"

Shame keeps us resigned to the darkness.

Shame convinces us that we cannot be healed as the Israelites were in the wilderness when Moses lifted up the serpent and all who looked upon it were saved.

Shame convinces us that it's not our deeds that are evil, but ourselves.

And shame causes us to misunderstand who Christ is. But listen to what He said: "For God so loved the world that He gave His only Son, so that everyone who believes in Him may not perish but may have eternal life."

"Indeed, God did not send the Son into the world to condemn the world, but in order that the world might be saved through him."

A man came out of the 8:30 service this morning and told me that a coach long ago told him not to go complaining about his problems to anybody because sixty percent of people don't care and the other forty percent are glad you're suffering. But that's not so with my Lord.

Our challenge is simply to accept that the road to healing is a road not of denial but of vulnerability.

The position to receive salvation is one of surrender.

Using Nicodemus as our model, we all must step out of the shadow and into the light not as we long to be but as we are.

In need!

Weak and broken, ready to receive healing, mercy, and acceptance from a loving Savior.

The hymn got it right: "We need not tarry till we're better or we will never come at all."

Come to the light – no matter how long you have walked in darkness, the darkness does not define you and you need not be afraid.

For anyone can be born again after having grown old – and everyone, no matter how old, is still in need of our Savior who makes all things new.

Amen.

The Greeks Wish to See Jesus
Luke 7:1-10 and John 12:20-33

This last week I was so glad to get to know our neighbors better. I had lunch with Father Roger Allen, the rector at St. James Episcopal Church, and Associate Rector, Daron Vroon, but before we went to have lunch, they gave me a tour of the church. Like us, they've been here for a while, and like us, they've seen some changes. The new sanctuary was built in the 1960's, and the oldest part of the campus is a chapel that predates the Civil War. In it is the third oldest working organ in the state of Georgia, and Father Roger told me that that very organ was torn apart by Union Troops, pipes filled with molasses, and thrown it into the street. That night, members of the congregation went out and collected the pieces, and eventually they were able to put the organ back together. A few years after the war ended, the organist was asked to play the reconstructed organ for a wedding. To be married were a nice Marietta girl and a Union Soldier. The organist agreed to play, but to make her true feelings plain, she wore all black to the wedding, and as the bride walked down the aisle, she played Chopin's Funeral March.

Isn't that story amazing?

Well, after the tour we went and ate sushi, and doing that so casually in Marietta, Georgia is amazing in and of itself. On the one hand, everywhere around here are reminders of two clashing cultures – you can't go anywhere in Marietta without thinking about the War Between the States. But on the other, there are the signs of cultures not clashing, but cooperating. Our historic square that's seen so much is also home to diversity, where we can eat food from the other side of the world. And that's good, because Southern culture isn't known for its sushi.

Think about all that we have access to because of the diversity of our community. Have you ever had a Mexican popsicle? You can get one down Roswell Road, and you should go try one because their popsicles are better than ours, just like French baguettes from that bakery on South Marietta Parkway (however you say the name) are better than the baguettes you can buy at Kroger.

Different cultures bring different gifts. I think that's true.

But to get back to the Civil War, what do the Yankees who come down here do better than Southerners? Nothing.

I'm just kidding. Mike Velardi told us last week about the menu he's preparing for when we host our neighboring churches for Holy Week daily noon worship and lunch. He'll be preparing Mootsarella sandwiches with basil and tomatoes for lunch, to go with soup, and I know that Mike's sandwiches will be more delicious than had they been made with regular old mozzarella.

Culture.

When you think of culture and our world's history of immigrants, civil wars, foreign languages, and foreign food, you know that culture brings with its gifts and resentments. That's why you can't just gloss over this week's significant detail in the Gospel of John. It's not by mistake that the Gospel of John tells us that these particular people who wish to see Jesus were Greek.

And what do you think of when you think of Greek culture?

First thing I think of are gyros, jy-roos, year-os or whatever you call them. But after that I think of this great culture whose influence is still obvious today. The gifts of Ancient Greece are Democracy, the philosophy of Socrates and Plato, the literature of Homer, and the medicine of Hypocrites. I remember my Greek professor in seminary telling us that she still believes that the literature of Ancient Greece has yet to be surpassed by any culture, and we learned to read Greek in seminary because this New Testament that we read from every Sunday was originally written in Greek.

Their language was the language of the world.

Theirs was the culture imitated across oceans.

They were the educated, the refined, and they possessed the great wisdom of the age.

Why then do they wish to see Jesus?

I've told you for the last two Sundays that the Gospel of John is full of important details, and this is important too. John doesn't tell us that these were foreigners or pilgrims, but specifies Greeks, and that means something.

It means they're not Roman, and that's interesting to think about. All over Jesus's neighborhood, since he was a kid, were Romans, but how many Romans wish to see Jesus? The only one I've been able to think of is that Centurion from our First Scripture Lesson, a Roman soldier who called to Jesus out of desperation that his slave might be healed.

Isn't that when we're most ready to cross those boundaries of culture and class? When we're desperate for help?

Consider the Greeks then. The age of Jesus was the age of Roman power and Roman rule. What was Greece but the Rust Belt? The "has been"? As the Roman star rose, so the Greek star faded, and what does that mean? That means that like the desperate Roman Centurion, the whole Greek nation was full of people who were ready to ask for help.

So, among those who went up to worship at the festival were some Greeks. They came to Philip, who was from Bethsaida in Galilee, and said to him, "Sir, we wish to see Jesus."

Philip told this to Andrew and then Andrew and Philip went and told Jesus. Why all the back and forth here? I don't know, but when they finally got to Him what did Jesus give them?

What did He offer these Greeks that no one else could have?

What was it that He gave that their own culture could not?

He taught them about death.

He told these Greeks, whose ancestors built the Parthenon which they had seen crumble that unless a grain of wheat falls into the earth and dies, it remains just a single grain; but if it dies, it bears much fruit.

Do you know how that radical teaching would have sounded to them?

I can't say for sure, but from time to time people seem to look at me with pity in their eyes, asking, "Joe, it must be a hard time to be a pastor at First Presbyterian Church. We've heard all about it. How the church split, and the membership declined, and the budget got cut. How are you doing with all that?"

People who ask these kinds of questions – they don't realize that when a culture or a church must face a time of desperation, it has been given the opportunity to reconsider its identity.

That when a church faces a hardship, her congregation is invited to stand and fight for what matters.

When people look on a church with pity, what they don't realize is that sometimes a grain of wheat must fall in order for new life to rise up and bear fruit – and so I tell them, "Every day is a joy and an adventure, because hope is alive, and God is good, and the Holy Spirit is at work shaping our church into something new."

And we can say that because we know that Christ changed the meaning of death.

He redefined hardship.

Christ flipped the meaning of suffering.

He transformed the grave – this dark place that all people throughout history have feared. He made it into the womb where ever-lasting life is born. But no human culture knows anything about that on its own, and only the desperate cultures go looking for such truth. Rome was busy crucifying criminals to preserve their power, because ultimately, that's what human institutions are all about – preservation of what is.

I think that's true. Consider the Greeks. In their hay-day, what did the Greek doctors want to do? Preserve life and extend it as far as possible.

The philosophers were only considering ways to live well while your heart was still beating.

Then you had Dionysus, the Greek god who said, "You're going to die anyway, so you may as well drink good wine while you can." What did the Greeks have as the Parthenon turned to ruin and the Romans rose to prominence while coopting their culture?

The Greeks were up a creek without a paddle, because it won't do you any good to preserve life or enjoy it when you're looking down the barrel of decline.

That's why Christ taught them about death. That's why He told them that through death comes new life.

Now that's a radical teaching for every culture.

And the next verse is even more radical: "Those who love their life lose it, and those who hate their life in this world will keep it for eternal life." What does He mean? He means that we need to think again about this way of life that we're fighting to uphold.

This reckless defense of gun rights. And this foolish idea that only gun owners are to blame. We can't be open to the Holy Spirit if we're so busy holding on to self-righteousness. Do we really want to hold on to the conviction that it's someone else's problem when children are dying?

Politicians can't fight for what's right if they're solely focused on re-election.

That's why our doctors must think not just about length of life, but quality of the life that we have left – for so often when we struggle blindly just to hold on to what we have, we are resistant to what God would give if we would simply let go.

Don't work so hard to save this life that you miss the invitation to something better.

C. S. Lewis wrote in his great book *Mere Christianity* that we are all like children, making mud pies in some back alley, and we are reluctant to accept an invitation to the beach. Too often we fight to preserve the life that we know, rather than accept God's invitation to something far better.

Those who love their life will lose it, sooner or later, no matter how hard they fight for it. All of what we have we will lose. That's just the way it is.

So, don't ever forget that that those who are willing to let go of their life in this world, who are working for something better, who are trusting God to provide a New Heaven and a New Earth, all of you will be like the child who leaves the mud pies of this present age for the ocean's bright sun and cool waves.

What must happen for all of us is this – we can't be confined to who we are, and we can't be fighting to preserve what we have now. Neither of those matters nearly so much as who He is and where He's leading us. Amen.

Here Comes the Bridegroom
Psalm 118:1-2, 19-29, and Mark 11:1-11

In the early service we sang, *What Wondrous Love Is This?* as the hymn to prepare us for those Palm Sunday Scripture Lessons that I just read. We sang:

What wondrous love is this, O my soul, O my soul.
What wondrous love is this, O my soul.
What wondrous love is this, that caused the Lord of bliss
To bear the dreadful curse for my soul, for my soul.

I hope you know that hymn. It's a good one, and it's about the saddest love song that you could ever sing. But sometimes it's the sad ones that get love right. And rarely is it the movies that get love right.

When Sara and I were first married we watched a lot of love movies that she picked out. It seemed like they all starred the same blond robot actors and followed the same plot line. You've seen these movies where boy falls in love with girl, boy chases girl, finally girl realizes she's in love with boy, but by then boy has moved on, so something dramatic must happen, and then everything ends happily ever after.

In these movies there's not a lot of compromising or arguing about money. No one really sacrifices very much, so I want to tell you that if you are looking for an example of real love, look not to the romantic comedies of this present evil age, but to the husbands who suffer through those movies because they love their wives that much.

Real love. Wondrous love — it's not like what you see in the movies, and if you want a glimpse of the kind of love that I'm talking about this morning, at the next wedding you attend don't just watch the groom to see if he cries as the bride walks down the aisle. Look at the father of the bride who is crying and has been for weeks. Real love, wondrous love, is full of this kind of sacrifice. The kind of sacrifice where you love her so much that you can give her away even though it tears your heart in two. But that's not what we make movies about. In movies, we invent these fantasies where two people complete each other without any work. Where dreams get fulfilled and where women are like genies who say to men, "Your wish is my command."

You think that's love? It's not, nor should it be — here's love:

When I was sinking down, sinking down, sinking down.
When I was sinking down, sinking down.

When I was sinking down beneath God's righteous frown,
Christ laid aside His crown for my soul, for my soul.
Christ laid aside His crown for my soul.

That's wondrous love. The kind with sacrifice. And that's what our world needs today. A few more people who are willing to lay aside their crown, their privilege, their power, their ego, for the ones they love. If you want an example of what that looks like, don't look to Hollywood, don't look to Washington DC, and don't try to find it on the Internet. The place you'll find wondrous love is in the Lord who comes to us this day with a steadfast love that endures forever, riding on a colt that has never been ridden.

Now, to slightly change the subject: Did you notice how He got that colt?

We read in our Gospel lesson from Mark that when they were approaching Jerusalem, at Bethphage and Bethany, near the Mount of Olives, He sent two of His disciples and said to them, "Go into the village ahead of you, and immediately as you enter it, you will find tied there a colt that has never been ridden; untie it and bring it."

To me, this is the funny part, because this is a weird request. But if you love someone, sometimes you'll do just about anything for them, be it sitting through a romantic comedy or becoming a horse thief! So, the disciples go, and He tells them, "If anyone says to you, 'Why are you doing this?' just say this, 'The Lord needs it and will send it back here immediately.'"

I wonder what those disciples said to that. "Yea, that will probably work Jesus. And why don't we stop by the bank to *borrow* some money while we're at it?" But if you love someone, you'll do things like this. You do things that you wouldn't normally do, because sometimes love is both joyful and humiliating. It's not all a walk in the park. Even a son's love for his mother requires a little bit of sacrifice. Let me tell you what I mean.

I have always loved my mother. So much that I'd even go with her to the grocery store. But you know what she would do to me? First thing she would do is drive around the parking lot looking for a good spot... for as long as it took to find one. Up and down we'd go. Then if someone was walking towards their car parked in a good spot we'd wait until they'd unloaded their cart, closed the trunk, buckled their seat belt. All the while I'm banging my head against the window.

I know the memories of that torture are still with me, because when I go to the grocery store today, I always park in the first spot that I see. Back then, I couldn't stand how she'd walk with her friend Cindy Dean for hours around our neighborhood going nowhere in particular, but she couldn't walk an extra 40 feet to get into the store.

It drove me crazy. Then, once we got in there things were good again.

She'd let me pick out whatever I wanted, within reason. No sugar cereal, but if I wanted to pick out a frozen dinner to have as a snack when I got home from school, I could. And we'd talk, walking down the aisles. "How was school? How are you doing?" And what she was asking was, "Joe, how are you really doing?"

This was a gift that I treasured. Even when I came home from college, I'd go with her to the grocery store. But then we'd finish shopping. We'd unload everything from the cart onto the conveyer belt at the register, and she'd run off leaving me there because she forgot the milk or something.

This sounds like a small thing now, because now I have money to pay for things, but back then the beep of each item being scanned felt like a countdown to my own execution. It felt like the clock ticking on a time bomb. Then when the last item would be scanned, the cashier would look at me. I'd tell her that my mom would be right back, and the cashier would just stare at me, and so would all the people in the line behind me.

Real love – you want to talk about real love, then you're talking about accepting some modicum of the inconvenience that she accepted for me. Real love is about making some sacrifices. Laying down your crown occasionally. But that's not how it looks in the movies, is it?

Real love is different, maybe even jarring.

I remember how shocked Sara the first time was I took her to meet my grandparents. Whether they loved each other or hated each other, I didn't always know, but I had gotten used to whatever it was. On the other hand, the first time I took Sara to meet my grandparents, they were already in the middle of a disagreement and my grandmother was so mad at my grandfather that she looked at Sara and said, "He's just a snake, I tell you. A mean old snake." That was Sara's introduction to my grandparents.

What was Sara thinking in this moment? I don't know, but it says something that she's stuck with me this long. She's perfect of course, but not everyone is, so marriage is hard. Relationships are hard. Friendships are hard, because loving someone means loving the whole of them, so sometimes that person whom you love is also the person who drives you crazy.

Ruth Graham, who was married to Billy Graham, is famous for saying: "I never considered divorce, though I often considered murder."

That's love.

And as my grandmother was dying in the hospital, I flew down to stay with my grandfather. We'd sit at the hospital all day while a ventilator breathed for her. Then at night, he'd just break in half, and would say things like, "I don't know what I'll do without her. Joe, I just can't believe this is happening."

That's love isn't it? He's a snake one minute and Romeo the next.

But if you want to talk about love, you must take both parts.

The Book of Revelation says that Jesus will ride like a bridegroom to join His bride who is the New Jerusalem. On this Palm Sunday we rejoice for He comes riding up to be with us, to take humanity as His bride, but consider humanity for a minute.

On the one hand, the Gospel of Mark portrays us as an adoring crowd, cheering, waving palm branches, and laying down our cloaks to pave the Savior's path. What's not to love?

But you know He could see beneath the cheers of an adoring crowd.

He had already predicted His death three times in the Gospel of Mark, telling His disciples that He would go to Jerusalem, be rejected, and be killed. He really knew us. He knew exactly what He was riding towards.

This bridegroom knew all that hid beneath our bridal veil, for He could see into our hearts.

What then did He hear as we cheered: "Hosanna! Blessed is the one who comes in the name of the Lord!"

Could He have smiled, knowing that soon enough the scribes, elders, and chief priests would stir us up so that we'd all be calling for His death? And yet He rides on. For us and for our salvation the Bridegroom rides on because that's what Christ's wondrous love for us is. He accepts the whole of who we are. He knows and understands the whole of who we are, and He rides towards us anyway.

That's wondrous love.

And if we are to love that way, we need to make some changes.

Maybe like you I read Darrell Huckaby in the Marietta paper, and a couple of weeks ago I loved what he wrote so much that I saved the article and recommended it to everyone I saw. Then, last Thursday morning he made me so mad that I threw the paper on the ground!

But that's what is required.

Jesus didn't ride into Jerusalem, realize that the place was full of Democrats, and turn around.

Before riding into the city He didn't first ask if any inhabitants were members of the NRA.

He didn't even fire the disciple He knew was going to betray Him, so how can we as Christians allow friendships to fall apart over issues that divide us?

If we used Facebook as Jesus would have used it, if in political discourse we used Him as our model, if we treated our neighbors the way that Christ treats us, then how would this world look?

For He knew us, everything about us, and still He rides towards us.

Today we remember that the Savior of the world comes to us like a bridegroom to be married to a people who will soon enough turn their back and call for Him to be crucified.

Why does He do it?

Because that's God's wondrous love for you and me.

Now, we must go and do likewise.

Amen.

He Will Swallow Up Death Forever
Isaiah 25:6-9 and John 20:1-18

In addition to being Easter Sunday, today is April Fool's Day, and I was reminded of that when early this morning, getting ready for the Sunrise Service at Kennesaw Mountain, I stepped into the shower to see that I was joined by the largest spider I'd ever seen.

The spider was plastic, but it's hard to tell the difference between a real spider and a plastic spider early in the morning.

And because it was early, as I was getting breakfast together, I didn't want to turn on too many lights, and I was just kind of feeling around the kitchen when my hand rubbed against a big old cockroach – which also turned out to be plastic, but I didn't know that at the time. It was still dark.

Both the spider and the cockroach were planted by our daughter Cece, and after all the commotion, I could hear her and her sister waking up. I decided that I'd just hide their Easter baskets and tell them that the Easter Bunny had decided not to come to see them this year.

I didn't really do that, but the point was made plain to me that it is easy to be fooled early in the morning. It's hard to see in the dark, so I can understand why Mary, who discovered the stone rolled away from the tomb that first Easter morning so long ago failed at first to understand what it all meant.

You noticed how the Gospel lesson began: "Early on the first day of the week, while it was still dark, Mary Magdalene came to the tomb and saw that the stone had been removed from the tomb." Now was just that stone enough to convince her that the Light was still shining?

Was this heavy stone rolled away from the mouth of the tomb enough to convince her that Hope was alive? That her Savior was risen from the dead?

As we read - no it wasn't - and that's because it's hard to see clearly when it's still dark.

So, "She came to the tomb, saw that the stone had been removed from the tomb, and ran and went to Simon Peter and the other disciple, one whom Jesus loved, and said to them, 'They have taken the Lord out of the tomb, and we do not know where they have laid him.'"

Isn't that something?

Just like a child who wakes up in the middle of the night, sees a shadow on the wall and assumes it's a monster, Mary saw the empty tomb and assumed someone had stolen her Savior's body.

When she first came to the tomb, while it was still dark, she saw the stone rolled away and jumped to the conclusion not that He had risen from the dead like He told them He would, but that some grave robbers had come along and stolen her Savior's remains.

And why would she think that? Because that's what we all do, for it's hard to see clearly when it's still dark. It's easy to be fooled early in the morning.

As I said before, we went out to Kennesaw Mountain this morning to preach a sunrise service. Libba and Wilkie Schell offered to give me a ride. Of course, I accepted, because that early in the morning I might have gotten lost.

I was preaching, wondering if my pants were on backwards early this morning. Why? Because it's hard to see clearly when it's still dark. It's hard to get dressed before you're really awake. Everything looks different. You make mistakes. You can't think straight, and everything seems just a little bit worse than it is.

Preachers used to tell newlyweds, "Don't ever go to sleep while you're fighting. Stay up and settle it before you go to bed," but the problem is that the more tired I am, the worse I get ... the more illogical and the less kind. If you ever need someone to make a mountain out of a molehill, wake me up at 2:00 in the morning, and I'll be sure to convince you that the world is falling apart.

Does it ever seem that way to you?

Guns in schools.

Self-centered politicians.

Bombs in North Korea.

Children going hungry.

Opium epidemic.

Human trafficking.

The list to prove that our world is falling apart just grows and grows.

And to make it worse, the news comes on in the evening after dark or in the morning before we are in our right minds, so it's hard to see the world clearly. Things seem so bad some days that it still feels dark even when it's noon.

But listen to what happened with Mary next.

Simon Peter and the other disciple went into the empty tomb that Easter morning so many years ago. They saw the linen wrappings lying there, and the cloth that had been on Jesus' head, not lying with the linen wrappings but rolled up in a place by itself. This is an amazing thing to see, but they don't see it clearly. It's still dark out, and so they just go on back home.

Look at Mary, on the other hand.

Mary stood weeping outside the tomb. As she wept, she bent over to investigate the tomb. As she wept, tears clouding her vision, she saw two angels in white, sitting where the body of Jesus had been lying. They said to her, "Woman, why are you weeping?"

You can just about answer this question for her.

Because He's gone, or so she thinks.

Because the only man who ever took the time to see her, and I mean, really see her, is gone.

Because the One who filled her with hope, who lit up the world with possibility, seems to be like a candle now burned out.

Had we been there to ask, she would have said, "I cry because I believed and now my doubts overcome me."

"Because I was found but now, I'm lost again."

"And because I just wanted to bury Him. But they have taken away my Lord, and I do not know where they have laid Him."

It's still dark out you see. She isn't seeing clearly, and that's understandable because it's hard for people to see clearly when the darkness of grief consumes them.

You can understand why she can't see the Light. It's still dark out and the shadow hasn't lifted, but then a man said to her, "Woman, why are you weeping? Whom are you looking for?"

Supposing Him to be the gardener, because it was still too dark out to recognize His face, she said to Him, "Sir, if you have carried Him away, tell me where you have laid Him, and I will take Him away."

Then, Jesus said to her, "Mary!"

Do you know what that was like?

To hear your name called?

In the shadow of a dark room, someone calling your name can be as uplifting as had they switched on the lights and all at once you can see clearly the truth.

Jesus said to her, "Mary!" and all at once the shadows lifted, the darkness was cast out, because the Light of the World called her by name.

But there were signs before that weren't there? Signs that she couldn't see because it's hard to see in the dark.

There's a truck that uses our church parking lot early in the morning and late in the evening. The owners park out there when it's still dark because they catch stray cats to spay and neuter. I'm glad that they do this, but late one evening someone drove up there because they thought it was a food truck. I wonder what they ordered, but my real point is this – it is still dark out there in our world today. It's still hard to see, but look out on the world, not with fear, but with faith.

Look for the stones rolled away, and when you see them, don't assume that your Savior's gone.

When you see His linen wrappings lying there, don't you dare just go back home giving up on hope?

And when you hear a voice, whether from a preschooler or a gardener, listen closely, for God is speaking still – during so much darkness God still speaks light to our shadow.

The Prophet Isaiah said it like this:

He will destroy on this mountain the shroud that is cast over all peoples,

The sheet that is spread over all nations.

For He will swallow up death forever.

The Lord God will wipe away the tears from all faces, and the disgrace of His people He will take away from all the earth, for the Lord has spoken.

And I say, He has done it.

On this April Fool's Day, the world can call us fools all they want. Still I say:

That He is risen!

He is risen indeed!

Amen.

I am Going Fishing
Revelation 5:11-14 and John 21:1-19

Last week for Spring Break, we took a big trip to Florida. We spent a few days exploring the Everglades, saw our fair share of alligators, and on our way home we spent some time at the beach outside Ft. Lauderdale. While we were there we ate breakfast in a little diner and in that diner one of the waitresses had the exact hair style that my grandmother had for all the years I knew her.

It was that classic look that requires you to carry a grocery bag in your purse to cover your hair in case of rain. My cousin Eric once proudly reported to his kindergarten class that his grandmother wasn't some old gray headed lady, which made my grandmother laugh, though she confessed that her red hair came from a bottle.

She died just a few years ago, but seeing the unnatural color of that waitress's hair and catching a whiff of her hairspray made my eyes fill up with tears. Now why is that?

Maybe you know.

Because sometimes you make a connection to people you've loved and lost at the strangest of times, though some of those times really aren't so strange when you think about it.

Maybe you feel something like what I'm talking about when you go to a baseball game. You sit down next to your grandson and you remember being his age and sitting next to your grandfather. Or you bake a pound cake using the recipe your mother scribbled out on an index card, corners now dulled, and ink smeared, but you wouldn't dare throw it away, would you? No – because to touch the card and to use the recipe is to travel to a different time. It's a link to someone you love.

You can think about fishing this way.

Here's a good fishing joke. How do you keep your Baptist friend from drinking all your beer when you take him fishing? Invite a second Baptist friend. I like that joke because it's about Baptists, but to my point: Fishing so often has nothing to do with catching fish. It has to do with relaxing or connecting. For fathers and sons or old friends, "Let's go fishing" is really code for, "Let's get away and spend some time together." Men can't just come out and say that, so they have to say, "Let's go fishing."

It's one of the many instances where the relationship between you and the person you do it with is far more important than the results. So when Peter says, "I am going fishing," just about all of us know it's not because he's hungry.

Peter goes to throw his nets back into the sea, because he wants to feel connected to the One who taught him how to fish for people.

Peter wants to breath the sea air, to rekindle his connection to the One who valued and redefined him.

Peter goes fishing because he doesn't want to lose the connection that he has with his friend and his Savior.

You know what I'm talking about.

That waitress with my grandmother's hair – it took some self-control not to hug her neck. All I did was place my order, but I wanted more.

I wanted her to tell me things that my grandmother never had the chance to say, and I wanted her to tell me things that she had said a million times before.

I wanted her to see our girls, to meet the grandchildren she didn't get to watch grow up.

And I wanted to tell her that I miss her, that I think of her, and that I'm sorry for the time when I called her the day after her birthday because I forgot to call her on the actual day.

You know, when people die, it feels like any chance you had of righting the wrongs is lost. When people die, to some degree you just must learn to live with regrets.

So, what was Peter thinking as he cast an empty net into the sea? You can imagine. With each toss of his net he was wrestling with the image of his Lord being led away in chains. Peter asked himself, "What did I do?" and answered, "I denied him."

One in a crowd asked Peter, "You are not also one of His disciples, are you?" And he said, "I am not."

You can just about hear Peter doing what people do when grief and regret assault the mind and the heart: "Just like he said I would, I denied him, I denied him, then I denied him again."

You can imagine.

It's hard enough to lose the people we love, but so often they leave us not only with grief but also with regrets. And such regrets can keep us chained to the past, never set free to really live out futures that the departed will miss.

So, he cast his nets without his fishing buddy, wishing for some forgiveness that a vast majority of the departed can't ever give, but not so with Jesus.

Peter was out there fishing, and the disciple whom Jesus loved spotted Him first.

The nets that had been empty were filled miraculously once again. Peter didn't see Him, but this other disciple pointed Jesus out, and Peter put on his clothes and jumped into the water. Isn't that interesting.

But that's the classic sign of shame and regret in Scripture. When Adam and Eve were ashamed, they made clothes from fig leaves because they couldn't stand before the Lord without inhibition. Possibly for shame and regret Peter covers his nakedness and jumps into the water in urgency. And once he reaches the shore, he is fed and set free.

You heard it: "When they had finished breakfast, Jesus said to Simon Peter, 'Simon son of John, do you love me more than these?'" Three times he asked him, and three times Simon Peter affirmed his love.

In the place of three denials came three declarations of love, and one road map for his future: Jesus said to him, "Feed my sheep."

Now, consider that, and imagine what do you think my grandmother wants from me?

To keep beating myself up about forgetting her birthday, or for me to remember all her granddaughters' birthdays?

What do you think any of the saints of light want from us?

To regret what's happened in the past, or to charge into the future?

And what do you think our Lord wants from us?

To beg forgiveness?

To cover our shame?

Or to feed His sheep?

We are all the time drowning in regrets. But did you see what Jesus did with Peter? In no time at all three declarations of love erased three denials, and immediately the one who escaped reality to go fishing and to polish his regret was sent out into the world with a new purpose.

Just like my grandmother would have done if she were still here, Jesus fed those disciples and He forgave them.

He filled up their nets one last time to get their attention. He prepared a meal for them on the beach. He let them know once again that washed in the water they had been made new. And then He put them back to the work of feeding sheep, getting them away from the work of self-inflicted regret.

If you go fishing for the same reason that Peter went fishing, I hope you have the same experience. Because you and I need to be feeding sheep, not feeding shame. But don't let me tell you how to do it. Don't let me lecture you about what you should be doing. I don't want to teach you how to fish.

You've heard it said: "Give a man a fish and he eats for a day. Teach him how to fish and he eats for a lifetime?"

That old expression has been revised by a writer named Roy Blount Jr.:

Give a man a fish and he must clean it.

Teach him how to fish, and you'll just make him mad.

But what if you feed him?

Jesus said to them, "Come and have breakfast." Now none of the disciples dared to ask Him, "Who are you?" because they knew it was the Lord.

Why?

Did He look like the Lord?

Did He sound like the Lord?

Did He dress like the Lord?

Or did He just act like the Lord?

Jesus did teach those disciples a lot about fishing, but more than that, He fed them. By this example He teaches us about feeding sheep.

Now let me tell you a story.

Last week my glasses broke.

More accurately, a screw fell out, and I broke my glasses trying to fix them.

I went into the optometrist. Georgia Eye Specialists, it's called. They're close by, but the Internet reviews have been hard on them, so I was suspicious. However, as soon as I got in there, I was convinced that this was a great place and I want to tell you why.

The nice lady who greeted me at the door and who was taking down my insurance information was eating skittles. This other lady behind the desk kept reaching into her little pile, stealing skittles one by one. A little annoyed, the lady taking my information looked at me and said, "You want one too?"

I did, so I took a pink one, and then I finished giving her my insurance information. She sent me to the part of the store where they repair glasses. I handed a young man my glasses, told him how I had broken them, sat down a little ashamed, and next thing I know, the lady from the front desk is coming to see me, offering me her very last pink skittle.

At this point I've decided that I have found the absolute best optometrist in the area. Why?

I have yet to see the doctor. I haven't had an exam, but they fed me. They fed me, and that makes a difference.

During Holy Week our kitchen volunteers fed at least 700 people who came to worship in our church.

Every Sunday morning and every Wednesday night the same thing happens, but they're doing a lot more than just feeding bodies – they're feeding souls.

And when I sat at the counter of that diner at the beach with my family, you know what I was thinking about? How many times I'd been fed by a lady with that kind of hairdo, which requires her to carry a grocery bag in her purse in case of rain.

How often she looked at me like I was the center of the universe.

How she would listen to me when I talked, with her full attention.

How she drove over for my freshman orientation because she was proud.

And how she'd call me darling, even when I wasn't.

Jesus fed them again, as He feeds us every communion Sunday, and then He sends us out to live our lives with purpose: "Feed my sheep," He told Peter.

Then He reminded Peter of what's true: "When you were younger, you used to fasten your own belt and go wherever you wished. But when you grow old, it will be different."

Don't spend any more time fishing for regrets.

Don't spend it on shame.

The clock is ticking.

So, feed His sheep as you've been fed.

Amen.

Part 7

Ordinary Time

Following the Season of Easter, the Church Calendar moves from fasting (Advent and Lent) and celebrating (Christmas and Easter) to what's called Ordinary Time. This liturgical season does celebrate major events in the life of the church, like Christ's ascension into Heaven (Ascension Sunday) and the day of Pentecost. Personally, during this season I celebrated my one-year anniversary serving First Presbyterian Church of Marietta, Georgia.

The Good Shepherd
Matthew 9:32-38 and Psalm 23

I wondered some about reading Psalm 23 in the King James Version. If ever there was something worth being able to quote from memory, this is it. And I think we should all memorize it in this translation, the King James Version, because it just sounds so beautiful.

But memorizing is hard for me, and for many of the members of my generation and younger. One of the problems with having information always at your fingertips is that you get out of the practice of committing information to memory. How many times have I said: "Why should I work to memorize it if I can just look it up on my phone?" But I find myself having to look up on my phone even my own phone number, which is weird, because I still remember the Buchanan's phone number that goes to a house they haven't lived in for at least 15 years. The landline of my closet friend from childhood is still right up here, but today, most everything just slips right out.

Why is that?

Part of it is because before we could google everything, we had to memorize it.

Before fancy cash registers, every fast-food employee knew how to make change. It's not that now people are dumb. It's that we slowly stopped using the parts of our brain that quickly retain information, and those memorizing brain cells got weaker and weaker, so other parts of the brain could get stronger. I don't remember all the facts and figures or technical language about the subject, but you can look it all up on the Internet.

It's true. And it's probably why some generations in attendance this morning didn't need to look at the bulletin to recite the 23rd Psalm while others did. And having the 23rd Psalm memorized is good, because cell service is bad in the Valley of the Shadow of Death. When you're walking through there, you must have some things committed to memory for them to light your way. You must know it. But we memorize less and less so our brains aren't used to it, and somewhere along the line, we stopped emphasizing memorization, stopped making sure that every child could say it by heart.

I think our confirmation class still must be able to. When I was in confirmation class here, I think we had to, but I'm a little rusty at reciting it from memory. Besides, saying the 23rd Psalm wasn't something that we did at home. It was something that I only worked on in order to join the church. A few generations ago, I don't think it was that way.

We used to memorize, but times have changed. Church has changed.

My grandfather once took us to the church he worshiped in as a child. He grew up in a place called the Caw Caw Swamp. It's somewhere in the Low Country of South Carolina.

His mother is buried there, and he showed us her grave. Then we walked into the little church, just one room to the place, and walking down the aisle memories were flooding back to my grandfather. One thing I remember is his saying, "On the back pew there, that's where the nursing mothers sat."

I remember how scandalized my mom was at the thought. She was sure it wasn't true, and misremembering is something my grandfather was and is prone to. But maybe she couldn't believe it because her childhood memory of church is so different. She often told me how she remembers playing with the head of her mother's mink during the worship service, and how if she weren't quiet, her mother would pinch her until she was.

That might be why when they first joined this church, they went to the service here that happened during Sunday School. We were young kids, and so we went to class. They could worship in peace, and I wouldn't have to get pinched.

Many churches have been thinking that way for at least the last 50 years: "Don't make the kids suffer through ... put them somewhere they can be kids." That's a thoughtful idea, a good idea in theory, but here's something that doesn't happen as much: the faith of our mothers and fathers getting passed down from one generation to the next.

That's a problem. We are slowly losing something, and sometimes I can see so clearly what it is that we're losing.

Have you ever asked a Presbyterian to pray? I've been to meetings where you can ensure that every Presbyterian will show up on time with the simple announcement: "Last one to sit down has to say the opening prayer."

You should hear my grandfather pray. Big, deep voice. "Let us return thanks," he'd say before Thanksgiving dinner. And I'll bet that he could do that because he had seen it done. As an infant in his mother's arms he heard powerful prayers in a one-room church before he even knew what it was.

Think about that one room church. As a toddler, there was no nursery for him to go to. They didn't even have Sunday School rooms, which isn't perfect, but how far it must have gone towards passing down our faith from one generation to the next. As much as I love and value Sunday School, being in one room to worship together matters. Being in the place where children watch their parents worship God matters, because the way they learn is by watching what we do.

And by "we" I don't just mean parents – I mean me and all of you. I mean everyone here who promised to help raise each baby who has been baptized in this church.

Do we, the people of this congregation, receive this child of God into the life of the church? If so, please answer, we do.

Will we promise, through prayer and example, to support and encourage her to be faithful in Christian discipleship? If so, please answer, we will.

That's what we do. No one ever says, "I will, so long as she isn't too noisy." Or, "I will, so long as she never drops a hymnal during the sermon." Every time we all answer, "We will." "Through prayer and example, we will support and encourage her to be faithful in Christian Discipleship." And it's through prayer and example, not mean looks and lectures, that we'll do it.

We model behavior to children, and when they're in here with us they learn to worship God as we do. Sooner or later, if they're sitting in here, they'll pick it up whether we're pinching them or helping them color. But if they're never in here, if they're always in the nursery or someplace else, they might not. That's because in the words of Rev. Joe Brice, the sage of Paulding County, "Worshiping God isn't taught so much as caught.

You learn to do it, not because someone told you how, but from being surrounded by people infected with the blessing that comes with worshiping God in Sprit and truth.

That saying "Do as I say, not as I do" doesn't usually work, does it?

So, if your dad sang the hymns, then I bet he never had to tell you to. But if he never cracked the hymnal, I bet that even if he told you to sing, you learned to do not what your father said to do but what he did.

If you heard your mother whisper the words of the 23rd Psalm, I bet you can hear her saying the words with you.

If your aunt held your hands when she prayed, I bet it stuck.

And if you saw your grandfather serve communion, it meant something powerful before you knew anything about Jesus and the Last Supper.

Rev. Lisa Majores told me that she felt a call to preach without ever really having seen a woman do it. Can you imagine how much courage it must have taken for her to try? To try something that you've never seen someone who looked like you do. She might say that her mother preached all the time, just not behind a pulpit. But still, it's so much easier if you've grown up seeing it done.

That's true of sheep too, and I know that because I've learned a thing or two about sheep. But not everybody has.

Last week Anna Grey Heart, our Preschool Director, arranged for a whole trailer full of farm animals to come to our church. The preschool kids got to pet them and hold them. There was a rooster as big as a four-year-old and there was a cute little pig. Betsy Sherwood told one of her students to stand next to the pig so she could take his picture. But he looked at her and said, "Ms. Betsy, that's a hamster."

If you don't know the difference between a pig and a hamster, you can't understand the 23rd Psalm, because to get a lot out of it you must learn some things about sheep. I googled "How do you train sheep to follow a shepherd?" and here are some interesting facts:

Even from birth, lambs are taught to follow the older members of the flock. Ewes encourage their lambs to follow. The dominant members of the flock usually lead, and if there is a ram in the flock, he usually goes first.[8]

Isn't that something?

Even sheep must be taught how to follow the shepherd, and they're taught by example.

We must show our kids to follow Him by following Him ourselves. And we must show them how to follow Him, because getting lost is just so easy.

From that passage we read in the Gospel of Matthew: "When he saw the crowds, He had compassion for them, because they were harassed and helpless, like sheep without a shepherd." Isn't that the state of things?

---

[8] http://www.sheep101.info/201/behavior.html

Like sheep gone astray, we often look for protection and guidance, and if not from the Good Shepherd, from any cattle thief who comes along.

Just as there is the Good Shepherd, there are plenty of bad ones in our world. I don't need to name names; you know whom all I'm talking about already.

There are people in this world who are leading sheep to the slaughter. Treating children like objects of desire, using their hands to strike fear and inspire shame rather than sow love. And these wolves in sheep's clothes are strengthened by our silence.

I believe it's significant that just before Jesus starts talking about people being like sheep without a shepherd, He gives a man back his voice.

He helps him to speak again.

And I say that this miracle is significant because there are people in this world whose power depends on our doing nothing.

There are men and women who want us silent, powerless, and irrelevant so that they can take whatever they want – but may the Lord give us back our voice.

This Sunday, we celebrate the work of the Interfaith Children's Movement and remember that April is Child Abuse Prevention Month. I hope you will notice again the picture on the cover of your bulletin of pinwheels surrounding the statue beside our playground. The Wednesday Night Children's Program, Mission Possible Kids, led by Alesia Jones, put the pinwheels there as a visual reminder that just as a shepherd cares for his sheep, we all play a role in ensuring happy and healthy childhoods for all children.

We are all sheep, cared for by the Good Shepherd, and we have an obligation to follow Him, so that the children of our church and our community will know whom to follow and how to follow. We must use our voices, our power, and our example to show the children of this world that the One who is worth following doesn't ask you to keep secrets.

He doesn't take from you until you're empty.

And He would never harm a hair on your head.

Instead: He restores souls.

Leads in paths of righteousness.

Provides, safety, comfort, and a hand to hold through the darkest valleys.

Let us show them.

By our example, let us show them how to follow the Lord.

Amen.

As He is, so are We in the World
Psalm 22:25-31 and 1 John 4:7-21

I was invited by a neighbor to go to a Braves game last week. He's a Mets fan, but that was OK. I can't say that I'm much of a Braves fan anymore any way. Dansby Swanson is the only player I can name. But there's more to a baseball game than the game. Anybody can tell you that. And now that the area around the new SunTrust Ballpark is so nice, there's plenty to do and plenty to spend money on, even if you're not a big baseball fan. So, we bought a drink and a $20.00 hamburger. We sat down in our seats, and even though I didn't know the names of the players on the team, even though I'd never been in this nice new stadium before, I immediately felt comfortable, because the rhythm of the baseball game is still the same.

Organ music plays before the game starts during batting practice, just like always.

The first pitch was thrown.

We stood for the National Anthem.

And when I heard the drum beats, it took me a second, but I remembered how to tomahawk chop and felt instantly at home, even in a new place.

In a church like ours, we call that kind of rhythm a liturgy. At certain times we stand up, sit down, bow our heads, give our offering. At no point do we do much of anything like the tomahawk chop, but my point here is that in this church, as it's true of so many places, there is a certain order to things; and in this place, the order matters.

However, I've heard it said more than once of our worship service, "I like the music and the sermon, but I don't really get all the other stuff." That's important to say. It's important to be honest, because walking into a Presbyterian worship service can feel like walking into hockey game or something. You don't want to ask someone what icing is, but when you do you find out that no one really knows. So let me tell you that the order we go by matters. Every Sunday, first we are called to worship God. We don't gather here to be comforted or corrected, to learn or be entertained. While hopefully all those things happen, what is of foremost importance is gathering here to worship God. God calls us to worship, so we emphasize that in the "Call to Worship" at the beginning. Right after that, we sing; then, we "Confess Our Sins", because coming into the presence of Perfection makes all mortals aware of our imperfection. It was that way with Moses, Jeremiah, and all of the others;

and so, it's true of us. But after we confess our sins, we are assured again of God's words of Forgiveness.

"Who is in a position to condemn? Only Christ, and Christ was born for us, He lived for us. Christ died for us. He rose in power for us. Christ prays for us." Consider all of that and be reminded that God is much more interested in forgiving us than we ever could have imagined.

Scripture makes it even more clear.

We don't read 1 John much, but its words are so beautiful and so clear: "God's love was revealed among us in this way; God sent his only Son into the world so that we might live through Him. In this is love, not that we loved God but that He loved us and sent His Son to be the atoning sacrifice for our sins."

Did you hear all that?

Thinking of the Parable of the Prodigal Son, the *Puritan Prayer Book* says the same thing:

I am always going into the far country,
And always returning home as a prodigal,
Always saying, Father, forgive me,
And thou art always bringing forth the best robe.

That's some Good News, isn't it?

But let's go back to our Sunday Worship Liturgy. You know what happens after we receive the forgiveness of God? We sing our thanks in the "Gloria," and then we are invited to "Pass the Peace of Christ".

If ever there was a misunderstood bit of worship liturgy, this was it.

Pastor invites the congregation to pass the Peace of Christ and I run off to make sure the Beadle has his prayer ready. One of the Deacons makes sure there's water in the baptismal font, and everyone else makes lunch plans for after the service. Those are all important things, but we're missing the point.

1 John says it this way: "Beloved, since God loved us so much, we also ought to love one another. No one has ever seen God; if we love one another, God lives in us, and his love is perfected in us."

We have a role to play; a role we are obligated to play.

Now, as a rule, I don't like it when someone tells me what I ought to do, but 1 John is right. If I've been loved and forgiven by God, how can I accept such grace without letting it flow right out of me and onto my neighbor? If I have such a keen grasp of just how imperfect I am, how can I reject another because of his imperfection?

And if no one has seen God, how then can we Christians make God known? With our love. That's what Passing of the Peace is about. The peace we receive – we pass on.

Mrs. Stephens taught us church kids to sing it in this church not so long ago, and Anne Maassen uses her songbooks still today. It's song number 55 in those little books they use:

We will walk with each other, we will walk hand in hand.
And together we'll spread the news that God is in our land,
And they'll know we are Christians
By our love, by our love.
Yes, they'll know we are Christians by our love.

Isn't that wonderful?

But these are bold words. While they are back in our hymnal now, they haven't been in a Presbyterian Hymnal for long a while, two editions or so. So, back in Tennessee at the church I served, the church secretary asked Mr. Lacy Coleman to carry all the hymnals to her desk so that she could paste the words to that hymn inside the front cover. Mr. Coleman had been the church custodian for 40 years, and he knew the congregation well. As he handed the church secretary the hymnals, he looked at the words to the hymn she was pasting, and he said, "So they'll know they are Christians by their love, huh? Well, you're sure not going to know these folks are Christian by how they talk or how they act."

That's not a good sign, is it? But it is an indictment of us all.

Certainly, preachers have tried to encourage their congregations to do better. Christians have been encouraging each other to get out there to be a light to the world, but it's hard.

Years ago, I was a part of the Fellowship of Christian Athletes at Marietta High School. Billy Graham was coming to Atlanta and was preaching the message "True Love Waits". We were handed these true love waits cards, and were sent into the school, armed with this message. As I went right up to this table of girls I hardly knew and handed out the cards, one of the girls pointed to her pregnant belly and said, "I guess it's kind of too late for me."

I threw the rest of the cards away after that, feeling like I had been sent out as a sheep to the slaughter, to say nothing of how I made that poor girl feel.

It's hard to know how we are supposed to be in the world, but back to our liturgy. At the end of the worship service, we follow the Acolyte out into the world as she carries the light of Christ, our Leader out there. And that's different from saying we go out into the dark world to take the light with us.

A group of young missionaries was at the airport with t-shirts that said, "Taking the light of Christ to Haiti." That's one idea, but here's the thing: what makes us think He's not there already?

The song I love so much says it differently: *And together we'll spread the news that God is in our land.* And 1 John says it like this: "As He is, so are we in the world."

That's what the Bible says. That's what the liturgy reinforces, but sometimes I am afraid we Christians think of God as being more in here than out there.

I led chapel for the preschoolers last Wednesday. I asked them about the baptismal font, to see if they knew what it was. One little boy said, "Jesus was born in there."

It's true that we gather to worship God in here.

We sing God's praises here.

We follow the liturgy in here; we read from Scripture. But Jesus wasn't born in here, nor is God confined to this place. And it's important that we get used to thinking that way.

The ancients were a little better about this than we are.

The picture on the cover of your bulletin is a 13th Century map of the world. We've sung before: "He's got the whole world in his hands." If you look closely to the East and the West, you can see His hands. To the South, His feet, and at the top, His face. Somebody looked at this map and said, "Where's the Big Chicken?" It's not on there.

According to the New Testament professor who showed it to many of us a few months ago, this map reflects the medieval worldview that Christ is a part of this world and God and God's creation are hardly separate. Just as we go out into the world following the Acolyte's flame, so Christ, already at work in the world, already a part of the world, will meet us out there and we Christians must get better about not being confined to the four walls of our sanctuaries.

I know that things have changed.

Sporting events used to begin not only with the pledge of allegiance but also with a prayer. Even school used to start with prayer. Some Christians have risen up in protest: "Bring prayer back to schools!" But I heard someone say, "As long as there are tests in school, there will be prayer in school."

I like to go eat at Gabriel's Restaurant, and when we were there a few days ago, I saw Wanda Reese walk in with her niece. I watched as Wanda took her niece's hand, and they bowed their heads to bless the meal. "You can pray just as well at a restaurant as you can at home," Wanda told me last Thursday, and she's right.

As He is, so are we in this world. That's what Scripture says, but we must live that way, for to quote the Apostle Paul in Romans chapter 8: "We are not as sheep led to the slaughter, but we are more than conquerors."

The Psalms say it too: "Posterity will serve him; future generations will be told about the Lord, and proclaim his deliverance to a people yet unborn, saying that he has done it." But too often we Christians live like maybe He hasn't.

We walk around with our heads low and our faith hidden beneath our coat as though our faith were something to be ashamed of.

Sometimes we treat our sanctuaries like bomb shelters – the place we go for protection – while treating the world like a trash can, as though the God Who created this earth no longer cared about it.

I'm not talking about evangelism this morning, at least not the way we've been thinking of it, because the only person who wants you to go knocking on doors less than you do is the person whose door you're about to knock on. Instead, what I'm talking about is the love that we know about, the love of God that we witness and hear about, running loose in our world. He is calling us to join Him. "As He is, so are we in this world."

I heard a story about a church in Syria this week. Paul Phillips and I got to have lunch with a man who supports churches all over the world, and he told us about this church in Syria. They have a preschool that serves families in the neighborhood. Late one night when the city was falling into chaos, troops moving through, planes in the air, the pastor rushed to the church to see it surrounded by armed Muslim men.

One approached the pastor, and he said, "Go home pastor. We will protect the church. Our children were students here. Go home; we will stay to protect the church."

God is at work in our world, changing and transforming lives. And as God has transformed our lives, we are now invited to join God at work.

As you go out into the world today, remember the liturgy, and may it give you comfort in an ever-changing world, reminding you of the thing that will never change: "As He is, so are we in this world."

Amen.

His Commandments Are Not Burdensome
Deuteronomy 5:1-21 and 1 John 5:1-6

There are some places in this world where I don't feel 100% comfortable, where I feel out of place, like I don't belong. One of those places is Michael's. I used the restroom in Michael's and I'll bet it is among the least used men's rooms in Cobb County.

But that wasn't the first place where I ever felt like I didn't belong.

Right outside Montreat, N.C. is a place called The Town Pump. Right away you can tell it's not for everybody. Sit at the bar, and it takes a while before someone takes your order. I was in The Town Pump with a pastor friend from Columbia, S.C., Amos Disasa, who was born in Ethiopia. I said to him, "Amos, I feel like I don't belong in this place." He looked around, "Joe, do you see anybody else from Ethiopia in here?"

This place, on the other hand ... I've always felt at home in this place.

That's the idea. This church isn't for some and not others. It's not for some genders and not others. This church isn't just for locals; it's a place for everybody because that's how the grace of God that this place stands on works. No one can earn welcome into God's house. None of us deserve it; therefore, all are welcome. That's how it's supposed to be, and that's how I know so many in the Confirmation Class feel. Many of you were raised here. Maybe you never felt new here because your parents have been bringing you here since before you can remember. And here, you were taught as I was, that God welcomes us with open arms and you don't have to do anything to earn it. You just must accept it.

But then one day, at the beginning of this school year, you showed up for Confirmation Class and we told you that in order to be a member of this church you had to do a whole bunch of stuff.

Bates Clarke asked his mom about that. "Why is it that you've all been telling me that God accepts me as I am, and then suddenly, I must memorize the books of the Bible, write a statement of faith, and go to all these Confirmation classes?" That's a good question. And I'm glad Bates asked it months ago, so I'd have time to come up with a decent answer by today. He's right. When you look at it that way I can see how Confirmation would seem like a sudden change, an abrupt shift from free welcome to fine print.

It's like when new members join the church and the first thing we do is hand them a pledge card.

That can feel like an abrupt change of pace – like we've invited you for dinner, then handed you the bill. That's not the intent of course, but it can feel that way.

In my mind this shift from free welcome to "now come pitch in" is something like the difference between celebrating the 4th of July and Cinco de Mayo. You might not know much about Cinco de Mayo. In this country it is a holiday celebrated mostly by margarita enthusiasts, a majority of whom I have a feeling have no idea what Cinco de Mayo even means.

Cinco de Mayo is a Mexican holiday that celebrates not Mexican independence from Spain - that's celebrated on September 16th – but rather Cinco de Mayo celebrates what happened after Spain was kicked out and Mexico gained independence. Mexican Independence was defended on May 5th, 1862, when the French, who sent a massive army attempting to take over the fledging nation of Mexico, were defeated. I looked all that up on the Internet.

Now most people aren't big on Cinco de Mayo (the 5th of May), but there is beauty not just in celebrating the gift of independence given by our forbearers, but also in celebrating our role in defending it.

The Apostle Paul says it well in his letter to the Galatians: "For freedom Christ has set us free. Stand firm therefore, and do not submit again to a yoke of slavery." But, we do. Sometimes we take for granted our freedom and forget that even today we must fight to defend it.

We are called not just to accept this Presbyterian Faith, but also to become a part of it.

Our Scripture Lessons make such a concept plain. From 1 John: "For the love of God is this, that we obey his commandments. And his commandments are not burdensome."

That might sound strange, because so often we think of being able to do whatever we want as defining freedom, but doing whatever we want isn't freedom at all. Consider those who resent being honest.

There's a Mark Twain quote on the wall of *Mary-Mac's* on Ponce de Leon, "If you tell the truth, you don't have to remember anything." Telling the truth is no burden when compared to the alternative, for those who lie must not only keep up with their lies, but they also become strangers even to themselves. In the same way, what could be so heavy a burden as hate? Some wise people have said, "Hate corrodes its container."

You want to see misery – think of the grimaced faces of the cold hearted. Think of the way withholding forgiveness destroys families. What is required of all of us who follow the Savior, calling us to love even our enemies, could hardly be called a requirement, for our path is the road to joy.

Therefore, because we Presbyterians do preach a message of grace and a salvation that comes free, it is critical to grasp the importance of the pledge card or the requirements of a Confirmation Class. These aspects of our faith are not contrary to the grace we proclaim, but stem from the Ten Commandments, written down by Moses from God, not designed to serve as penalizing measures in life, but rather as guidance for how to live a joy filled life.

"Honor the Sabbath day and keep it holy." Here is a commandment that is more defiled than any other. We defile it because we don't believe that our salvation is contingent on our obedience to it, and indeed it is not. Instead what is at stake is the condition of our hearts - literally. Think about it. No, God will not strike us down for going into the office on a Sunday; God will not need to, for the 80-hour workweek brings with it its own punishment.

His commandments are not burdensome, especially compared to the weight of sin.

And as God did our ancestors, so the Lord calls us now to live the Christian life and to participate in the work God is doing. In Deuteronomy we read: "The Lord our God made a covenant with us at Horeb." Not with our ancestors, but with us. He's talking about all of us who are alive today.

God gives the gift to us. It's ours, but we can't just accept the gift; we must defend what we've been given and make it our own.

We, who feel at home here, are invited to make others feel welcome so that this church never feels like Michael's nor the Town Pump, but like the Master's Table where all are treated like honored guests.

For while we all are honored guests at the Master's Table, too often we are only mindful of our own comfort or discomfort, forgetting what it's like for the friend sitting next to us.

He invites us. But remember, we are also disciples, called to serve, making this faith our own.

The knitting you saw out in the Gathering Area will go out into the world because we don't just receive God's warmth and welcome, we can give it.

Think of that and know that on the one hand is free grace, and on the other is joyful obedience.

Neither are burdens. Both are gifts.

So, Bates Clarke, Confirmation Class, Congregation, Joe Evans ... remember that we are not only defined by the gifts we receive freely. We are defined also by our response – how we live – what we fight for. And this faith, this church ... this is worth fighting for.

Amen.

Lifting His Hands, He Blessed Them
Psalm 93 and Luke 24:44-53

Today is a significant day on the Church Calendar as well as the family calendar. I hope you remembered that today is Mother's Day, but in addition to this being Mother's Day, today is also Ascension Sunday, and what we just read from the New Testament book of Luke is how Jesus said goodbye to His disciples as He ascended into heaven. We read: "Jesus led them out as far as Bethany, and lifting His hands, He blessed them. While He was blessing them, He withdrew from them and was carried up into Heaven."

It sounds as though no one remembered exactly how He blessed them, what kind of blessing it was, just that as He said goodbye, as He was carried up into Heaven, He wasn't leaving them with one last instruction, one last piece of advice, but with one last blessing.

I've known people who left me with a blessing.

One is a man named Jim Hodges. He was the chair of the Associate Pastor Nominating Committee who interviewed me for my first position as a pastor. It was Good Shepherd Presbyterian Church out in Lilburn, and after the committee that Jim chaired interviewed me and picked me out of the bunch, I was honored to serve that church by preaching about once a month and trying my best to be a pastor while making a whole lot of mistakes.

There were plenty of mistakes. One Sunday, moving through the liturgy, I skipped right over the children's sermon. On occasion, I'd ask everyone to stand when they were supposed to sit down. Regardless, every Sunday I preached I'd give the benediction, would walk out of the sanctuary by the center aisle, and as I walked, to my left, there was Jim Hodges giving me a thumbs up as though I had done a great job.

I had served that church for about two years when Jim was diagnosed with lung cancer.

I went to visit him, and those visits were like many where I was the one being comforted rather than providing the comfort. For a long time, I watched him fight, but finally the doctor told him he was near the end. He called and told me. The next day I walked into his hospital room. His wife Carol left to give us privacy, and I asked Jim if he was scared.

His answer: "I'm not sure Carol has a good understanding of the heating and air maintenance contract. Other than that, I just don't quite know what I'll do when I see Him."

"See who Jim?" I asked.

He kind of stared off and said, "Will I laugh? Will I cry? When I see Jesus, I don't know quite what I'll do."

In the next day or two, stuck in his hospital bed, he took a picture of his thumb, had Carol get it developed, and gave it to me. It's framed and on my desk. Jim is telling me that regardless of how I'm actually doing, he thinks I'm doing just fine.

Now that's a blessing, isn't it? But not everyone says goodbye with a blessing.

Today is Mother's Day, and ideally, what we celebrate today are our mothers who loved us and blessed us. But not everybody's mother was like that.

Some mothers are abusive. Others neglectful. At the very least, I think most of us have felt at one time or another as though our mother's love language was criticism rather than praise. Do you know what I mean?

Maybe it was your wedding day. You were about to walk down the aisle, and your mama came to see you to say, "You look beautiful honey, but I can't help thinking that you could have lost five more pounds."

On the day of graduation, maybe you remember, that there were plenty of mothers who just cried. Out of joy or pride, they couldn't even speak, but maybe yours could: "Congratulations," she said, "But I can't help but wish you had graduated with honors like your friend Peter. Isn't he a smart one?"

Last week I heard from a little league baseball coach, a good friend of mine named Davis. And Davis told me that at the coach's training they were presented with an interesting finding that when polled, a majority of major league baseball players when asked the question, "What is your worst memory of sports from your childhood," say, "The ride home from the game."

Most parents want their children to succeed. Most mothers want their children to be successful, but too many of us believe that for our children, the road to success and independence is paved by criticism and advice rather than blessing.

As a preacher I've received my fair share of critique. It hasn't all been thumbs ups that are for sure. In my third year of seminary, the development office sent a group of us to Jacksonville, Florida to promote the school. I was proud to have been asked to go and rode down with the group. I stayed with my mother's cousin Sonya Harrell who lives down there. I preached at this Presbyterian Church and as the congregation left, I received many handshakes and encouraging words, but for the last man in the line. I remember he was wearing a three-piece suit.

"What year are you in the seminary?" he asked.

"I'm in my third-year, sir," I answered.

"Nearly three years?" he said, "Well, they should have taught you something better than that by now."

And he was on to something. But men in three-piece suits, mothers and all the rest of us, we all need to remember that as Jesus ascended into Heaven he didn't say to His disciples: "You've been a Christian for how long now? You sure ought to be doing it better by now."

That's not how it ends. Those aren't the last words — the last words are a blessing.

A blessing from God to you, because regardless of what your mother said or failed to say, the words you heard in your baptism are trustworthy and true:

"You are mine," says the Lord, "my beloved, and with you I am well pleased."

Too often we Christians walk around like we've just been to the dentist: "I should be better; I should do better; I should floss more." But today we remember the truth: that as the Lord ascended into heaven, He left giving an imperfect group of disciples his blessing. Today it's no different for you or me.

Consider how the service ends. This service today and every service here ends with a reminder of the main thing:

The Lord bless you and keep you.
The Lord make his face to shine upon you.

We leave this place as those disciples left Bethany, knowing that the Lord ascended into heaven giving us His blessing and that matters because you can't change until you know you're worth it.

You can't be redeemed until you believe that you're worthy of redemption.

You can't be saved until you know it in your heart that you are worth saving.

No mother is perfect.

None of us had the mother that said everything we needed to hear. And those of us who are mothers today will take comfort in this truth as well. We all must allow Christ to fill in what others left empty, to heal what others broke or left broken.

So, these are good words to end on and these are good words to remember:

May the Lord bless you and keep you.

The Lord make His face to shine upon you, and give you peace, and give you peace.

Amen.

Prophesy to These Bones
Ezekiel 37:1-14 and Acts 2:1-21

On this Pentecost Sunday, I am reminded of my Aunt Beth's fear of snakes. My Aunt Beth once told me that she's deathly afraid of all kinds of snakes – live snakes, dead snakes, and sticks that sort of look like snakes. You could try to tell her that a Rat Snake isn't venomous, or you could hold up the black piece of hose to show her that it's just a hose, but it doesn't matter. That's because we interpret reality based not just on what's actually there, but on what we think we see.

Sometimes fear colors our vision, other times it's anxiety, sometimes love keeps us from seeing clearly what's actually there. And that's why on that Pentecost Day long ago when the Holy Spirit came to the Disciples, not seen by all, not everyone reacted to it the same way.

We just read: "Divided tongues as of fire appeared among [the Disciples]. All of them were filled with the Holy Spirit and began to speak in other language as the Spirit gave them ability." If ever there was an obvious miracle, an obvious encounter with the Divine, this was it. But listen to how the people who saw it responded: "All were amazed and perplexed, saying to one another, 'What does this mean?' But others sneered and said, 'They are filled with new wine.'"

You see, we are a people who mistake sticks for snakes and disciples for drunks.

Sometimes its fear that colors our vision, other times anxiety blinds us to everything but our worries. Sometimes a kind of pessimism or heartbreak keeps us jaded and far from seeing a miracle that appears right before our eyes.

That's true today, and it's always been true.

Think back to Moses leading the people across the seabed on dry ground. Was there anyone among them who saw the waters part and said, "I'm not walking through there. Leave me with the Egyptians." Did anyone who watched David defeat the giant Goliath sneer and say, "That's the luckiest kid I ever saw." The answer is – of course they did. Miracles happen every day, and people walk right past them.

If my Aunt Beth can mistake a stick for a copperhead, then of course, we can mix-up a miracle and a coincidence, scoff at a movement of the Spirit.

Miracles happen, but are our hearts attuned to see them? Not always.

Back in Tennessee there is a homeless man named Melvin. Columbia, Tennessee is a small town, and everyone there knows Melvin. He would sit out in front of the church, waving to cars that passed by. People would honk and wave. More folks than you'd imagine would stop and give him money or food, and all that was fine with the people of First Presbyterian Church because Melvin was outside. The problem came when Melvin started coming into the church.

Now these are good Christian people, and they welcomed him with open arms. But you get too close to a homeless man who hasn't had a bath in weeks or months and hospitality gets demanding. At some point in the summer, when sweat compounded body odor, someone said to me, "Joe, either he takes a bath, or I have to stop coming to church. I just can't take it."

That sounds like a simple enough request – to ask a man to bathe before he enters the Lord's House. But there were legends about Melvin.

That he was scared of water because his parents drowned.

That no one could get him to bathe because smelling bad protected him from thieves who would steal his money.

There were all kinds of stories, so when I went over to ask him about taking a bath, I thought I knew already what he was going to say. Still, I said, "Melvin, you know I love you coming to our church, but I need you to do me one big favor. I need you to take a bath." I was so sure that he would say no that when he said yes, I didn't know what to do!

I had just spat the words out and expected that that would be that – my plan went no farther. When he said," Sure Joe, I'll take a bath," there came the problem of what next – and despite my surprise at his willingness, I was smart enough to want to strike while the iron was hot. I suddenly remembered that the Methodist Church across the street had a shower, so I ran over there, asked Valarie at the front desk for access to the shower, not knowing what she'd think, but fully expecting her to say no. Instead, she handed me a key to the church, and out from under her desk she just retrieved a bag with clothes, a bar of soap, and shampoo, as though she had been preparing for this exact moment.

How do you explain that?

Coincidence?

Dumb luck?

If among the crowd on that Pentecost long ago were those who sneered and said, "They are filled with new wine," then today we are wise to remember that our entire culture is poised to reinforce the cynical assumption that nothing is getting any better in this world and that to believe differently is foolish superstition. But listen to this: There's a little girl in Club 3:30. You know Club 3:30 is the after-school program led by Mary Groves that meets here at the church. This little kindergartner came to our afterschool program from a region in Central America so remote that she had never before sat in a chair. Not only that, this region she was from was so remote that she didn't speak English or Spanish, but an indigenous dialect. That was the beginning of the year. Last month the Kiwanis Club of Marietta gave medals to the teachers of our city schools, charging them to recognize students for whatever accomplishment might not typically be recognized. This little kindergartner came to Wednesday night supper wearing a medal that she told me was for the most improved English speaker in her kindergarten class.

Now there's a miracle.

One that happened right here, in this room … but it won't tell itself.

In our world today, this fear filled, prejudice prone, fake-news kind of world where everyone, it seems, is tailoring facts to protect their agenda, we Christians must be prepared to stand and speak with feet planted firmly in the truth.

On that Pentecost long ago it was Peter, standing with the eleven. He raised his voice and addressed the crowd, "These are not drunk as you suppose, for it is only nine o'clock in the morning. No, this is what was spoken by the prophet Joel: 'In the last days it will be, God declares, that I will pour out my spirit on all flesh.'" That's what Peter did, and if we don't get in the habit of doing the same, so many will just walk right by, focused on the next worry that comes along. For everywhere there are people looking out on the world, taking in what they see through a lens of fear … people who hide from the world, drowning under the weight of headlines. The defeated ones who allow death to have the final word, treating hope like a fairy tale. Then, in desperation so many put faith in the makers of empty promises, forgetting the power of God who breathes life into to dry bones.

In our First Scripture Lesson we read: "The Lord said to the Prophet [Ezekiel], 'Mortal, can these bones live?' He answered, 'O Lord God, you know.' Then the Lord said to the Prophet, 'Prophesy to these bones, and say to them: O dry bones, hear the word of the Lord.'"

Christians, we are called to see the world through the lens of faith, remembering the power of God that gave dry bones new life, the power of God that turned Moses's staff into a snake, divided the waters, and who still sets slaves free; the power of God that gave the boy David a strength greater than the giant, who granted the king victory, and gave his son wisdom; the power incarnate in Christ who walked out of the grave conquering sin and death, defying the authority of empire, entrusting fishermen with the most important news ever heard.

Whenever we read the paper or watch the news, too often it is a different message, an empty message that causes us to retreat in fear and react in apathy. But God is still at work in our world, and Satan, that liar, cannot change this reality. He can only shape our perception of it, causing us to see drunks rather than the mighty prophets of God, coincidence rather than His mighty hand, decline and defeat rather than triumph and victory.

Prophesy to the bones then.

In a world in conflict over issues of race, point to the gospel choir that sang for a prince's wedding, and remember that regardless of those who fight it, change still comes.

In our world of violence, prophesy words of hope, reminding teachers and students, parents and grandparents, that no matter how many shootings there are, death will not have the final word; for born within each graduating class is hope for a better future, and those who stand against it might as well get out of the way.

We, the church, must prophesy to the world – for our world is quick to forget that the Holy Spirit Who was alive on Pentecost so long ago is at work still, is alive and awake still. So, as we go out into the world, armed with pizza boxes full of tools for evangelism and mission prepared by our Children's Ministry Director, Alesia Jones, let us be bold to see it and celebrate it.

Amen

This Treasure in Clay Jars
2 Corinthians 4:5-12 and 1 Samuel 3:1-10

This account I've just read of the young prophet Samuel is one of the most influential stories ever told. Even if this were the first time that you've heard 1 Samuel chapter 3 read, I'm sure it's not the first time you've heard this story.

As is true in all its retellings, in 1 Samuel there's a boy, a virtual orphan, who was left at the Temple by his mother who loved him but couldn't keep him. She left him at the Temple and as she did, she sang a song about the mighty hand of God Who will bring justice. We suspect that he remembered the song, and that he sang it to himself, because it lived on. Its themes are all through Mary's "Magnificat" that she sang while she was pregnant with Jesus. But the song Samuel's mother sang that Samuel remembered, while powerful and memorable, couldn't protect him from everything, even if it warmed his heart on cold dark nights.

This boy Samuel was raised by an old man named Eli who was in charge at the Temple. Eli had two wicked sons. They took what they wanted, as though everything was theirs. You can imagine it. It was the definition of unfair. As Eli's sons ate what they wanted, even eating the meat that was to be offered to God in sacrifice, you can picture young Samuel sweeping the floor and saving the crumbs. He wore only a linen tunic his mother made for him. He slept not in a bedroom, but on the Temple's cold floor. You know this story.

You know it because it's not at all different from the story of another orphan, left on the doorstep of the home of a Mr. and Mrs. Dursley who lived on Privet Drive. They had a son, Dudley, who had more birthday presents than he could count on both hands, and a second bedroom to store all that his parents gave him. But where did little Harry sleep? He slept cramped in the closet under the stairs just as Samuel slept on the bare Temple floor.

You know this story.

It's like that of James, whose parents died in an automobile accident involving an escaped rhinoceros. He was sent to live with these two horrible aunts, and while he knew the sea was nearby, he was confined to his yard where an ancient peach tree eked out its meager existence. The tree, like James, didn't die or give up – no, but it struggled. Despite the struggle, in time, that measly tree grew a peach so large that James crawled up into it and lived out as great an adventure as you can imagine.

You see – you know this story. You love it, because it embodies hope, and you want it to be true. If you know the story well then you know that the one who has the hardest time believing this story could ever be true is the little boy who finds himself right in the middle of it all.

From 1 Samuel we read:

At that time Eli, whose eyesight had begun to grow dim so that he could not see, was lying down in his room; the lamp of God had not yet gone out, and Samuel was lying down in the temple of the Lord, where the ark of God was.

Then the Lord called, "Samuel! Samuel!" and he said, "Here I am!" but ran to Eli, and said, "Here I am, for you called me." But [Eli] said, "I did not call; lie down again."

Now why did the boy Samuel assume that this voice calling him was Eli, his old guardian, and not God?

That's like asking, "Why wasn't Harry Potter patiently awaiting his acceptance letter to Hogwarts School" or "Why wasn't James checking the old tree daily, waiting for his escape peach to grow." Like both Harry and James, Samuel assumed that it was the old man who was calling him because he had long ago learned his place in this world – long ago he had learned that while some people are destined for greatness, others are destined to sweep the floors.

While some people are born into privilege, it is the lot for others to have to accept the scraps.

While God calls some people, while God has something to say to some people, while God has important work for some people, the bullies of the world had taught young Samuel that scrawny boys like him are wise to accept his meager lot.

It's a shame, isn't it? How many people, young and old, accept the lie the world tells as the truth, but some are blessed to be waked up.

That's what happened in the *Sword and the Stone*. That great Disney movie in which a young boy named Arthur, unable to fill up his hand-me-down robes, can barely carry the sword of the knight he serves as page, and it's no surprise that this young boy – you remember, they call him Wart – forgot the knight's sword back at the inn. Only in desperation does he pull the sword from the stone, a legendary feat that only the chosen king was prophesied to be able to do.

When Wart finds out what it means that he's pulled the sword from the stone – that he's the one destined to be king of England – he's the most surprised of anybody. Why? Because the world had given him his name and his lot – he'd accepted both, because those who sleep under the stairs can't help but assume they deserve it.

On the one hand, there are some people who are born on third base and assume they've hit a triple, but others who make their bed in the ash heap and assume they too should go out with the trash. Because of the way they are talked to, the way they are addressed, the way they are treated, some assume it's best to be satisfied with their meager lot.

Did you know that they called her Cinderella because without a proper blanket, she made her bed in the smoldering coals, and the cinders burnt holes in her dress?

But there's more to life than the house of an evil stepsister and her spoiled daughters.

There's more to your identity than the hard words you've been told, for as hard as they may be, words can't define everything or everyone, and it is God who said, "Let light shine out of darkness." So, Samuel's story continues:

The Lord called Samuel again, a third time. And he got up and went to Eli, and said, "Here I am, for you called me." Then Eli perceived that the Lord was calling the boy.

Therefore Eli said to Samuel, "Go, lie down; and if the Lord calls you, you shall say, 'Speak, Lord, for your servant is listening.'"

So Samuel went and lay down in his place.

Now the Lord came and stood there, calling as before, "Samuel! Samuel!" And Samuel said, "Speak, for your servant is listening."

Can you imagine? Can you imagine what this scrawny, beaten down boy must have felt in that moment?

Perhaps he felt like the little boy on your bulletin cover. Playing marbles in the dust, only to look up and see that he's on the moon.

It reminds me of Dr. Sam Matthews, who just retired from First United Methodist Church. He was pastor there for the last 15 years, and despite all the conflict that marked the beginning of his ministry there, today First United Methodist is the largest church in Marietta.

He took me out to lunch once, and he told me that sometimes people will ask him if he had ever dreamed he'd one day be the pastor of such a large Marietta church. He said, "When I was growing up I couldn't imagine myself serving any church - not one of the small country churches I grew up going to, and certainly never would I have dared imagine serving this one."

You can't help but imagine the same kind of thoughts were in the minds of those disciples who brought the message to the first Christians in Corinth, for there in 2 Corinthians we read:

We have this treasure in clay jars, so that it may be made clear that this extraordinary power belongs to God and does not come from us.

Now Samuel already understood that, because it is easy for the Samuels, the Harry Potters, the Jameses, and the Cinderellas to remember that their treasure is a gift. But those evil stepsisters – they speak from entitlement, greed, and envy – and rather than fan the flame of hope, they try to put it out.

Like Scout's teacher, Miss Caroline, in *To Kill a Mockingbird* ... she was from Winston County in North Alabama, and she looked down her nose at her pitiful first grade students, especially the one who had no need for her Winston County charity.

Scout told it like this: *As I read the alphabet, a faint line appeared between her eyebrows, and after making me read most of My First Reader and the stock-market quotations from the Mobile Register aloud, she discovered that I was literate and looked at me with more than faint distaste.*

This teacher reminds me of the man who sat with his back towards the preacher at the royal wedding two weeks ago. Because the sermon didn't come from him, he couldn't even turn his head, though those were mighty words proclaimed by Bishop Michael Curry.

The opposite of that man's demeanor was that of Andrew McIntosh last Sunday as Joe Brice preached at the 8:30 service. As Joe went on about the buzzard that hit his trailer, and the kindness of a mechanic, you should have seen Andrew listening. It was as though Andrew was thinking: "I know this guy lives in Paulding County, but he has something to say!"

Now that's the truth. And we are all such clay jars. Inside our mortal flesh is treasure, and the reason we tell this story again and again – this story of Samuel, the boy prophet, called by God – is because it is our story too. Like him, we have known those who see only the clay jar, overlooking the treasure. But not so with God!

So, while all the wicked stepbrothers and stepsisters believe that the world is their oyster and they're free to take whatever they want, remember that whether you believe you deserve nothing or everything, you're wrong – because we aren't extraordinarily special or extraordinarily plain – we are clay jars containing a treasure.

We are disciples entrusted with Good News.

We are slaves who serve the Master.

We are guests at the table of the King.

We are mortal flesh, blades of grass, but within us burns the Light, though it is not ours.

Like Paul and the disciples in Corinth, regardless of what we have heard from those who have pushed us down, we must live knowing that within our clay jar, our feeble frame, is a treasure that can change lives and set the world on fire.

Amen.

Israel Demands a King
2 Corinthians 4:13-5:1 and 1 Samuel 8:4-18

Last Sunday, right after church, we headed to the beach. It was a short trip, just for a few days, but it was great. We were in Florida, a very nice place to be this time of year, plus, while we were there, we spent time with good friends, rode waves, ate fried shrimp, and climbed to the top of a 125-year-old lighthouse. But the highlight for me happened when we walked out on this jetty.

A jetty is sort of like a peer, in that it enables you to walk out into the ocean. It's lower to the water than a peer, and is mostly made up of great big rocks. On this jetty, on top of the rocks, was a nice, flat sidewalk, with the rocks on either side, and when we got to the end of the sidewalk, we stopped, leaned against the railing, feeling the ocean breeze, and looked around at the fishing boats coming into the bay to our right. Then we noticed to our left a small crowd of people, maybe a dozen, gathered around the railing, looking at something in the water. Someone said: "There are three of them," which got our attention, so we walked over to where everyone else was looking, and there they were – three manatees swimming in the water, eating seaweed or something off the rocks.

It was one of those times where I felt like I was in a movie. I just couldn't believe what I was seeing, and our girls were struck as well. They didn't say anything – they just watched. They were spellbound as these huge tails came out of the water like they belonged to mermaids. Their noses would come up to take a breath, and they have these kind faces that make you smile.

A woman named Laura in a bikini was so moved by their appearance that she climbed the railing, navigated the rocks, and eased into the water to touch one on the back. You might wonder how I knew her name was Laura. That was because her boyfriend or husband shouted: "Laura, if they eat you, can I have your cigarettes?" But we could all understand why she went down there to get close to them. It was an unforgettable moment. A gift from God!

And even though it only lasted for a few minutes, it was enough to make an impact. As the manatees swam away and the crowd kind of broke up, without thinking and to no one in particular I said, "that was amazing." Laura overheard me, and she said, "Thank you."

"Uh, I wasn't talking about you, Laura," I wanted to say, but didn't.

That's what I'm focused on this morning, because I wasn't talking about Laura's being amazing. I was talking about God's majestic creations. I was

240

commenting on the beauty of the earth, the majesty of the sea, not the woman who patted the manatee on the back.

But that's humanity for you.

God creates the world, invites Adam to name the animals, and next thing you know, Adam's walking around like he owns the place.

God sets the planets in motion. With a word, there are tides and days, sunrise and sunset, but leave it to us to say, "Thanks God, but we'll take it from here. You might have made the manatee, but I can touch them, so let's hear it for me! Look how many likes my selfie with the manatee got on Facebook."

Even in the midst of a miracle, sometimes we humans find a way to be naïvely arrogant about our place in the world. There used to be a framed sign on the wall of Bill and Louise's, now Louise's, that said:

Teenagers! Tired of being hassled by your stupid parents? Act now. Move out, get a job, pay your own bills…while you still know everything.

Now, teenagers pushing parents out of the way is nothing new, but ego can get the best of all of us. We all have thought that we knew better than anyone above us, such as a boss or a supervisor, and some of us have even thought that we knew better than God. We read in our Second Scripture Lesson:

When Samuel became old, all the elders of Israel gathered together and came to Samuel and said to him, "You are old, and your sons do not follow in your ways; appoint for us then, a king to govern us, like other nations."

This displeased Samuel, and Samuel prayed to the Lord, and the Lord said to Samuel, "Listen to the voice of the people; for they have not rejected you, but they have rejected me from being king over them."

This is a historic moment in the history of Israel. Up until this point, the nation had been governed by judges. Rather than a centralized government, they had been a nation of tribes, but now the people demanded a king because they had a better idea than the system God put in place. They want to push God aside and put one of their own on the throne.

Such a moment in history begs the question: "Just who do they think they are?"

God brought them out of slavery in Egypt by a mighty hand, sent down the commandments to order their life, provided them a land flowing with milk and honey, but now it's: "Thanks God, but we'll take it from here."

241

And we know how this is going to turn out, because the tragic story of human power is still playing itself out.

A family was on a long car ride to the beach, and to make conversation, a little girl asked her mother if she'd like to meet the President. Mom said that she'd be honored to meet the President someday.

"But what if it were Richard Nixon?" her daughter asked.

"Then forget it," her mom responded.

This response seems typical. Depending on partisan bias, there are those presidents who we revere and others who we'd not cancel a dentist appointment to meet. At times and to varying degrees, we see their feet of clay, but the problem isn't just the perceived flaws in a person. The greater problem is our bad habit of expecting humans to do things that only God can do.

The Lord said to Samuel, "Listen to the voice of the people; for they have not rejected you, but they have rejected me from being king over them."

That was one of humanity's worst ideas, because people are just people. The president is a person elected to high office. We might call him King James, but even LeBron can't win the NBA finals on his own. It doesn't matter whether you're a Kennedy, a Bush, a Kardashian, or even King David, you cannot fill God's shoes.

This morning David is painted on the cover of your bulletin. While robed in grandeur, the Prophet Nathan points to the skull of Uriah the Hittite whom David had murdered, illustrating in plain terms the reality that human power is just that - human. Not one of us is immune to corruption. Absolute power corrupts absolutely.

That's the truth, but age after age, we press on in foolishness, pushing God out of the way. So, God relents:

"Listen to the voice of the people in all that they say to you; [God said to the prophet Samuel] for they have not rejected you, but they have rejected me from being king over them."

Every time we take the weight of the world and put it on our shoulders or trust the fate of our nation to some other frail human being, we follow in the footsteps of these Israelites who though freed from slavery in Egypt, willingly submitted again to a yoke of slavery by calling for a new Pharaoh who goes by a different name.

The Lord and the Prophet tried to warn us: "These will be the ways of the king who will reign over you ... he will *take* your sons ... he will *take* your daughters ... he will *take* the best of your fields."

He will take, he will take, he will take – six times the prophet describes what this king will take and not one mention of what this king will give. This speech is without qualification or exception. A king who takes is the only kind of king that there is, because if "Laura of the Manatees" naturally assumes center stage, pushing God out of the way, what will these humans do with absolute power, day in and day out? Like David, they will look out from the palace, and will see what they might take as their own.

A group of Church leaders has recently authored a new confession of faith. It's not too unlike the one that we'll use this morning after the sermon for our affirmation of faith, as this new confession is but a reminder from 21st century Christian leaders of the sovereignty of God over human power and authority.

Article 2 of this new confession, called Reclaiming Jesus and inspired by among other things the #MeToo movement, rejects the violent abuse of women, and states: "We lament when such practices seem publicly ignored, and thus privately condoned by those in high positions of leadership. We stand for the respect, protection, and affirmation of women in our families, communities, workplaces, politics, and in our churches." This kind of statement must be made again, in the 21st century, because the powerful of every time and place are prone to take, and this taking begins with ego.

So, we have to be careful. I have to be careful.

You know, every once in a while, someone will walk in here for the first time and will say to me, "Pastor, this sure is a beautiful church you have here."

You know what I say? Call me Laura, because every time, "Thank you," I say, as though I could take credit for this ... but it's hard to give credit to one we can't see.

Those disciples who brought the gospel to the church in Corinth were wise, and they gave credit to God anyway:

"We look not at what can be seen but at what cannot be seen; for what can be seen is temporary, but what cannot be seen is eternal. For we know that if the earthly tent we live in is destroyed, we have a building from God, a house not made with hands, eternal in Heaven."

Now isn't that a wonderful thought? In light of our world today, let us be bold to consider the house not made by human hands, for even now it is all around us.

The day after we saw the manatees, I could see it.

I walked out on the jetty again, thinking that this time I would be like Laura and I would jump in the water too, but the manatees weren't there. Instead, I saw a group of kids on surfboards learning how to ride the waves.

Our power is limited. We are but blades of grass, but the Creator, Redeemer, and Sustainer who causes the waves to rise and fall, invites us to ride the waves.

To worship the Lord and enjoy Him forever.

To bow our heads before Him, and to allow Him to share our heavy burdens.

What a blessedness, what a peace is mine, leaning not on my own power, relying not on human power, but leaning on the Everlasting Arms.

Amen.

Open Wide Your Hearts
2 Corinthians 6:1-13 and 1 Samuel 17:32-49

Our girls joined a swim team this summer, so last week we attended their second swim meet. This was the second swim meet I'd ever been to, so I was going into this without knowing exactly what I was getting into. Initially I thought that these things would be like every other kid's sport – I thought we'd watch them swim for 45 minutes, then go eat ice cream – but swim meets are different from the other sports they've played.

At last week's swim meet, the first race we had a child in was race number three. That was good. We got to the pool, immediately saw some action, but the last race we had a child in was race number 78. With a swim meet, we're talking about a four-hour commitment.

A lot of waiting.

A lot of just passing the time.

A lot of parent watching, and you know there are different kinds of parents at a kid's sporting event.

There's the worried parent, whose kid is trying to get over to the starting block, but she just keeps applying more and more sunscreen.

There's the still at work parent, who missed his kid's race because he got a call from the office.

Then there's the overly chatty parent – who missed her kid's race because she was talking – but worst of all is the dreaded phenomenon of the parent who is way too into his kid's race, yelling, cheering, videotaping.

Like a zoologist, I was observing all this, but this being our second meet, I was also trusted with a job. I was supposed to record who came in first, second, third, and fourth for all these races. That meant that I, along with all the other parents who had jobs, went to a training in the clubhouse. In the training, the swim-meet official added fuel to the overly competitive parents' fire by saying, "This is my favorite age to officiate, because one of those kids we see swim today could be a future Olympian. I've seen it happen."

As she said that, you could see some parents put their chest out a little bit.

I like kids' sports, and I like a lot of the lessons that kids who are in sports or other competitions learn. After all, life is a struggle, so I think it's important that kids learn to work hard and try their best. But thinking back to those parents hoping their child is a future Olympian, I worry about those parents who put too much hope in their kid's athletic ability because sooner or later they will all line up on the block next to a Michael Phelps – some guy with four-foot arms and flippers for feet, and when he leaves everyone behind in his wake, what will they do?

You know, I bet Goliath's daddy would have loved kids' sports.

You saw him. You've heard about him.

The measurements listed in Scripture are ancient. 1 Samuel tells us that Goliath of Gath's height was six cubits and a span, and the weight of his coat of mail was 5,000 shekels of bronze. The shaft of his spear was like a weaver's beam, and his spear's head weighed six hundred shekels of iron. We don't have the conversions down exactly – but know this: he was far bigger than everyone else at the time. Depending on whose conversion chart you use, and which scroll you base your conversion on, Goliath was either 6, 9, or 12 feet tall, carrying around a spear whose tip weighed at least 15 pounds. That's amazing!

Imagine that. Imagine what that giant would do to a soldier with a spear tip that weighed 15 pounds.

But really, he didn't have to do anything with it. It was scary enough just seeing the man carry that thing around.

Every day for 40 days Goliath stood before King Saul's army and taunted them, saying: "Today I defy the ranks of Israel! Give me a man, that we may fight together," but no one was ready to step up. No one wanted to face him. They just looked at him and his spear. Then they looked at the spears they were carrying around and sheepishly walked back to their tents, questioning their manhood.

His spear tip weighed 15 pounds. That must have been sending everyone to the blacksmith for a bigger spear tip – because that's how we think. We have to win, and if winning means investing in some better equipment, so be it.

You might have read what Darrell Huckaby wrote in the paper last Thursday. The changing cost of baseball was the title. He reported that the new median price for a kid's baseball bat is $250. That's really something, isn't it?

But that's human.

Maybe you remember the good old days when you could just use your big brother's hand-me-down bat. I remember that my Dad had saved his wooden bats that he used when he was a kid. He even had this crooked one that he said was special for hitting curve balls – but I wanted the kind of bat that everyone else had, so he took me to a sporting goods store. They had a whole selection of bats, and I picked out one of the flashiest ones they had – bright colors, cool logo.

I could hardly swing it, but that's beside the point.

If the other team has their own batting helmets and bat bags, then we want them too.

Give us swim caps and racing goggles.

If their football team practices all summer, then we had better do the same.

Uniforms, gloves, bats, shoes.

Weight lifting, private coaching, traveling from one state to another.

Drink Gatorade, eat a Power bar, spit sunflower seeds.

In sports it's all bigger, better, faster, stronger, so we were all standing around the pool – and one mom kept yelling to her daughter: "Dig, dig, dig!" And I want our kids to dig too.

I want them to dig deep and do their best. But when they dig and dig and hit rock bottom – I want them to know who can get them out.

The 12 Steps of Alcoholics Anonymous begins:

First – We admitted we were powerless over alcohol – that our lives had become unmanageable.

Second – We came to believe that a Power greater than ourselves could restore us to sanity.

Those are two powerful lessons. Two steps that human competition in sports, school, music, or business would never push us to take.

To come in touch not with our strength, but our powerlessness.

To depend not on ourselves, but on a power greater than ourselves. If we can't do that, then what will we do when we face the great challenges of life?

247

There are giants out in our world that we can't outswim, no matter how hard we dig.

Daemons that we can't outrun no matter how hard we train.

Challenges that we can't push over no matter how much we work out.

There are giants out in our world that just we can't beat on our own, and that's where the lessons we learn in sports and every other human competition come up short. That's exactly where the lessons we learn here in this place have the power to save.

I've known those who have faced giants: lawsuits, cancer, unemployment … times when it didn't matter how nice a person was or how hard he worked, because these were *giants* these people were facing – and Giants are Merciless!

Night after night, and day after day, it was as though the giant was standing before them saying, "Come to me, and I will give your flesh to the birds of the air and to the wild animals of the field." And when they felt as though they were all alone, some of them looked within themselves, saw that what strength was in their mortal body was insufficient, and knew they were defeated because hope stopped at the summation of their own power.

But David - David knew that he was not alone, and so he looked not within himself, not at his feeble frame, but to the mighty power of God who had saved him before and would save him again.

He said to King Saul: "The Lord, who saved me from the paw of the lion and from the paw of the bear, will save me from the hand of this Philistine." Then he said to the giant: "You come to me with sword and spear and javelin; but I come to you in the name of the Lord of hosts. This very day the Lord will deliver you into my hand; so that all the earth may know that there is a God in Israel, and that all this assembly may know that the Lord does not save by sword and spear; for the battle is the Lord's and he will give you into our hand."

David put his hand in his bag, took out a stone, slung it, and struck the Philistine on his forehead, proving to all us mortals, that there will always be someone bigger.

There will always be someone faster.

The paper tigers will roar and the giants will rise up, for in this life there will always be challenges too big and enemies too strong – depression, addiction, hatred, ignorance, or middle school, just to name a few. All these times where it is easy to feel so all alone and oh so small before forces that could crush us. But as the giants taunt us, we are not alone – don't forget that.

Remember that at the limit of our human strength is the mighty power of God.

From 2 Corinthians we read that through great endurance, in afflictions, hardships, calamities, beatings, imprisonments, riots, labors, sleepless nights, and hunger, these Christians endured not by digging or fighting through. These hardships could not be powered through or outrun. They endured by purity, knowledge, patience, kindness, holiness of spirit, genuine love, truthful speech, and the power of God; [they were] sorrowful, yet always rejoicing; as poor, yet making many rich; as having nothing, and yet possessing everything, because like David they trusted in something outside themselves.

Like every man and woman who defeated their own personal Goliath – they turned, not inward, but upward.

They stopped fighting, to pray.

They remembered to use the words of columnist Leonard Pitts, "[God's truth] will blast through [human power] like a comet through a sandcastle, and giants can taunt, intimidate, pressure, and boast in their own power – but they are nothing before the mighty power of God who makes the sea waters rise at his command and listens to the cries of his children in trouble, regardless of whether they are documented or undocumented."

The poet John Milton said it like this:

When I consider how my light is spent,
  Ere half my days, in this dark world and wide…
Thousands at his bidding speed
  And post o'er Land and Ocean without rest:
[But] They also serve who only stand and wait.

Open wide your hearts – and remember that when you pass through the deep waters, you are not alone.

When you pass through the rivers, they will not sweep over you.

When you walk through fire, you will not be burned.

For hope begins when we recognize the power greater than ourselves.

Amen.

For Your Sakes He Became Poor
2 Corinthians 8:1-15 and 2 Samuel1:1, and 17-27

The Fourth of July is this week, and so today, in preparation and anticipation of celebrating our nation's birthday, our hymns for worship, especially the last hymn, are a little more patriotic than usual, which makes sense. This church of ours not only makes its home in the United States of America, but Presbyterians were in this country from the beginning. I'm sure you've heard it said that there were more Presbyterian signers of the Declaration of Independence than any other denomination. If you see any Baptists or Methodists this afternoon, be sure to remind them of that.

So, this week I've been thinking about how more than 200 years ago Presbyterians declared independence from England and her king – and how quickly and definitively the line between the mother country and her colony became a battle line.

How the Declaration of Independence was like a Dear John letter to say, "We'll be getting along better without you."

How after the Boston Massacre, British soldiers were seen as enemies who could not be trusted.

How the Boston Tea Party violently expressed the resentment of American consumers.

How, at that time, British sympathizers were tarred and feathered by mobs made up of their own neighbors.

I think about all that, for today I see the same kind of rift that steadily grew between America and Britain spreading to divide America against herself.

On Friday June 22, Sarah Huckabee Sanders, press secretary, and defender of President Donald Trump, walked into a little 26-seat restaurant called the Red Hen in Lexington, Virginia. The chef of the restaurant called the owner, Stephanie Wilkinson, at her home, telling her that the staff was a little concerned. What should they do? Ms. Wilkinson left her home, drove to her restaurant, met with her employees and said to them: "Tell me what you want me to do. I can ask her to leave," and they said "yes."

Stephanie Wilkinson then politely asked the press secretary to leave, and the Press Secretary did.

I would have left too. After all, if the chef and wait staff didn't want her there, who knows what they would have done to her food, but that's not the point, is it?[9] The point is that on the eve of the Fourth of July, it's obvious that the citizens of our nation cannot eat at the same dinner table.

That's a big deal.

And while I suppose we've always been divided or dividing, there's always been a difference between Republicans and Democrats. It seems to me that this is a newly challenging and confusing time. But, as Christians, in times of challenge and confusion, if we are wise and faithful, we turn not to Twitter, Facebook, or to whatever we consider to be the real or fake news, but to Scripture where there is always guidance and hope.

In this season of division, where compromise seems impossible, and party loyalty seems paramount, we turn this morning to the transition of power from one king to another in Ancient Israel to see how God's chosen conducted himself in a time of conflict.

We turn to David, who was chosen by God and anointed by the Prophet Samuel long before he had the chance to sit on the throne and rule. He had been waiting and waiting. Only now is he finally poised to sit as King of Israel, for King Saul is dead.

Effectively, this is exactly what David wanted. This is what any of those who were close to Saul and knew his paranoia first hand were waiting for too – the nation was ready for a new king, and possibly David was more ready than anyone. But as David hears about Saul's death, will he celebrate? Will he pontificate? Will he boast in his own superiority over the leader he is to replace? Will he play up Saul's weakness or highlight his mistakes?

Will he add fuel to resentment, make a monster out of the former king and tell Israel, "Now that I wear the crown, everything is going to be perfect"?
No.

The messenger who delivered the news of Saul and his son Jonathan's death is killed, not rewarded, and rather than dance on the grave of the dead King Saul, Scripture tells us that David intoned this lamentation:

Your glory, O Israel, lies slain upon your high places!

---

9 https://www.washingtonpost.com/news/local/wp/2018/06/23/why-a-small-town-restaurant-owner-asked-sarah-huckabee-sanders-to-leave-and-would-do-it-again/?noredirect=on&utm_term=.5a403c8833f7

How the mighty have fallen!
Saul and Jonathan, beloved and lovely!
They were swifter than eagles,
They were stronger than lions.
O daughters of Israel, weep over Saul,
How the mighty have fallen in the midst of the battle!

It's hard to imagine some politicians doing something like that today.

Maybe you remember the presidential debates a couple of years ago. Someone asked the candidates Donald Trump and Hilary Clinton to say something nice about the other. A man named Carl Becker stood up and said, "My question to both of you is: regardless of the current rhetoric, would either of you name one positive thing that you respect in the other?"

It was one of the most awkward moments I've ever seen on television.

Today I'd love to hear President Trump sing a song about the former president the way David sang about the former king, so I wrote a couple verses. Imagine President Trump singing this:

He could beat me in basketball.
He has a great head of hair.
The way I've criticized him, hasn't always been fair.

It's hard to imagine something like that happening.

On the other hand, as the Marietta Daily Journal covered the death of long-time football coach James Friday Richards, I read a quote from Scott Jones, who started the Kennesaw Mountain High School football program in 2000. He referred to Coach Friday as the comrade of coaches and said he acted not only as a coach but also as father figure to everyone. Now he said that although Coach Jones had only one win against Richards' Marietta teams in all the time they played against each other. Jones said, "Richards was always generous before and after their games — win or lose. He was a competitive coach who wanted to win, but in the grand scheme of things, he was not all about that."[10]

It seems to me that considering politics in the United States of America today, in the grand scheme of things we are exactly all about winning.

---

[10] http://www.mdjonline.com/cobb_football_friday/cobb-coaches-and-players-reflect-on-a-life-well-lived/article_2c093ef6-7883-11e8-96ba-934104f7846f.html

Politics today seems to be a zero-sum game, where the only thing that matters is winning. Prioritizing winning, using the chosen method of pretending to lead by pointing fingers rather than together looking for solutions, puts us the people in great danger.

The great Hubert Humphrey, who served as Vice President under Lyndon Johnson, is quoted as saying: "To err is human. To blame someone else is politics."

That's funny, but in this country today we are tearing at the seams. Friendships are ending, crowds are chanting, fingers are pointed. It has become commonplace for some to express their discontent not in words but in bullets, and our leaders can't seem to pull us together to do anything about it.

Every news cycle, it becomes progressively harder to imagine those on one side of the aisle sitting down for a meal with those on the other, and that's bad because sitting down for a meal together is one of the most powerful opportunities we have to see those who think or act differently as people.

Let me tell you what I mean.

I once worked with a big group of men and women of questionable citizenship status. I was a lawn maintenance man, and as one of few among the group with a valid driver's license, I was quickly promoted to crew leader.

One morning driving to the shop, I noticed that a rabbit ran out into the street and the car ahead of me hit it. A few minutes later, as I was loading the mowers and weed eaters into the truck, one of my crewmates, a man from central Mexico named Miguel, rode into the shop on his bicycle. One hand was on the handlebars, the other holding a dead rabbit by its hind legs.

He skinned the rabbit, cleaned it with a hose, and then he asked me to stop by his apartment on the way to our first job, so he could put it in his refrigerator.

This was one of those jobs where they didn't want to pay us overtime, so when we had made 40 hours by Friday morning, they sent us home early and Miguel invited me over for lunch at his apartment.

I was nervous, but I reluctantly accepted. Fortunately, rabbit tacos were not on the menu. Over the lunch table, I learned a lot. I learned that six of them lived in a one-bedroom apartment so that they'd have more money to send home to their wives and children. I learned that only one of them knew how to cook, because all of the others had left wives and mothers back in Mexico without learning how. I learned that back home they were professionals. One was a dance instructor but they all had come to Atlanta in the hopes of providing a better life for their loved ones.

That's what I learned at that table, and that's what I hope for in our country. I hope for such a table even more than I hope for a song – I hope for a table around which our whole country can sit and get to know each other again.

A table where people overcome differences and see each other not according to label – not as legal or illegal – republican or democrat – but as a child of God.

In this church there is a table.

You remember whom He ate with – tax collectors and sinners, fishermen and Pharisees.

He even calls on us to come and eat with Him, despite our questionable status, despite our guilt.

Having been invited by Him despite our depravity, we must be bold to live up to such a gift of radical and undeserved graciousness.

What they said to the church in Corinth was: "For our sakes, He became poor," so who do we think we are, keeping it all to ourselves?

For our sakes He became human, so who do we think we are, pretending that we're any better than anyone else.

For our sakes He gave up His life – that's what this table is about – and you and I are invited. But if we receive this grace, we had better be prepared to pass it on to our neighbor who doesn't deserve it either.

David was generous to Saul though Saul was trying to kill him.

And Christ is generous to us, and He invites us here.

But ... we must be as gracious to our neighbors as Christ has been to us.

Amen.

Whenever I Am Weak, then I Am Strong
2 Corinthians 12:1-10 and 2 Samuel 5:1-5, 9-10

In the past two weeks, as is often the case, I have come to a better understanding of my personal failures and limitations.

I had a meeting at *Cool Beans Coffee Shop* on the Square with David Eldridge, pastor of StoneBridge Church, and David wanted to introduce me to another pastor who was in there – it was pastors's day at *Cool Beans*, I guess. The other pastor that David wanted me to meet had just started at Roswell Street Baptist Church. I shook his hand. His name was Mark, and in the course of his introduction, I suddenly realized that this was the very Mark who had been trying to get in touch with me. I had failed to return several of his messages. He had been emailing me to see if I might be interested in this new initiative he's getting started.

Has this ever happened to you? The very person you've been avoiding, either intentionally or unintentionally, is suddenly right in front of you?

David said, "Mark, this is Joe Evans at First Presbyterian Church."

I added, "The guy who has failed to return your messages."

Then he said, "Don't apologize. You're not Jesus."

Isn't that the best response?

I've been thinking about how I might use that phrase, because it's such a freeing reminder of the truth. Of course, I know I'm not Jesus. None of us are, but that truth doesn't always keep us from trying to be perfect.

In reality, we're limited. Fallible and forgetful. But we don't want to be. In fact, we're often actively trying not to be. So, I'm grateful to this Mark, because he helped me face the reality that I'm just me though I often want to be more than me. I want to be King David. Don't you?

In our Second Scripture Lesson from the book of 2 Samuel, David's accomplishments are listed:

David, who already had been embraced by the Southern Tribes, now unifies the nation by gaining the esteem of the north as well.

He made a covenant with the Elders of Israel.

He was anointed king.

He captured the ancient city of Jerusalem, established it as the City of David, and then built it up.

Scripture also mentions that he does all of this by the time he turned thrity.

But here's the main thing. In verse 10 we read: "And David became greater and greater, for the Lord, the God of Hosts, was with him."

With this simple verse it becomes clear why David was able to do all of these things by the time he turned thirty. It was not because of his own strength that he became great, but because the God of Hosts was with him. Should we continue to review the reign of David, future years would show that when he forgets this vital fact that God is with him ... when he fails to accept the limit of his power and steps beyond to seize more than he has right to, his great story turns from victory to tragedy.

The human condition is that even the greatest of us is limited, and one of the beautiful gifts of our faith is to be able to embrace our limits not with resentment but with gratitude.

Paul said it like this in our First Scripture Lesson: "On my own behalf I will not boast, except of my weaknesses." He then goes on to describe without specific detail the thorn, which keeps him from being too elated. "Three times I appealed to the Lord about this," Paul wrote, "that it would leave me, but he said to me, 'My grace is sufficient for you, for power is made perfect in weakness.' Therefore, I am content with weaknesses, for whenever I am weak, then I am strong."

That's a hard truth to accept, but it is truth.

I recently heard a philosopher describe Superman. The writers of this comic book ran out of stories to tell about him, and his popularity began to wane until they introduced kryptonite, the mineral that zaps the super hero's strength. They revealed a weakness. Of course, we would all like to be super heroes: strong, fast, ageless, beautiful.

We might long to be the perfect mother, the sole provider.

We want to wake up early, exercise, walk the dog, feed the family, then go off into the world prim and proper, witty and informed, caring and concerned, and I know that's true, because when we have the chance to project our image out onto the world, we show the Facebook Community not the truth but what we want the truth to be.

Our children must make good grades, make the cheerleading squad, and act in the school play, while attending to grandparents, looking grownups in the eye, minding their manners, and writing all thank you notes no more than four days after their birthday party.

That's what many of us want from our children because we hold ourselves up to such high standards. Success in life demands rising to the high standards set by culture, but what about the moment when we run into our own Mark, who wrote us an email that we've failed to respond to for days or weeks.

Will we then rejoice in being reminded that we aren't Jesus? And don't have to be?

Or will we promise to try harder to be perfect in the future?

A requirement of having faith in God is not having absolute faith in ourselves.

That might sound strange, but if we could do it alone, what need for God would there be?

When Paul says: "Therefore, I am content with weaknesses, for whenever I am weak, then I am strong," he is reiterating a point that he's made several times before: that if we could be perfect, what need would we have for God's grace?

If we could master human existence, going through life without making mistakes or if we could rise to every occasion without the need for God's sustaining hand, then why believe?

If perfection were ours, if holiness were something we could work for and eventually gain, if it were possible for us to rise to every challenge without ever falling or failing, then what did Christ die for?

Therefore, we are better — far better — when we know our need, for then we can give thanks for our Shepherd who supplies it.

We are mighty — not when we are strong enough to do it ourselves, but when we must lean on the ever-lasting and almighty arms of our Savior.

When we remember our blindness, then we can give thanks to the One who opens our eyes.

And when we know what we can't do, then we can trust the One Who can.

Children who grow up believing that it all rests on their shoulders – who forget how to play, and spend their vacations at the beach studying for the ACT – we worry about the pressure that they're under but don't know what to do about it, because we adults can be just as bad.

We adults, who live into the lie … the idolatry that the future rests in our hands … are to be pitied for foolishly trying to carry a burden that already rests in our Savior's hands.

Too often I try to carry it myself.

After all, I am the new pastor at First Presbyterian Church of Marietta, Georgia.

I've now been proud to call myself your pastor for nearly one year. This summer is the one-year anniversary, and daily I'm thankful to be here among you. Being your pastor has its many perks. Sometimes I'm recognized by people I haven't met. I was having breakfast at Come–N–Get It and the man at the register whom I've only met once or twice before called me by name. "Thank you for your business Rev. Evans," he said. This was an occasion for my head to expand.

Only later did I realize that I was wearing a nametag.

I'm still me, you see – and you're still you.

The struggle is to accept such limitations, and even to rejoice in them. For it is in recognizing our weakness that we are more fully Christian, and less failing superheroes.

I'm sure that you've heard by now that a Long-Range Planning Committee has been formed at our church and that members have been meeting, organizing five task forces to strengthen our church's technology and communication, as well as our youth group, preschool, and Club 3:30 after-school program. They've focused on these areas because you, the congregation, talked more about these five areas than any other. You know already that God is alive and at work in those places, and to be a stronger church means joining our God where God is already at work.

We've adopted this statement to guide our work: "First Presbyterian Church exists to change and transform lives with faith, hope, and love" – and it sounds obvious, but it's worth saying that the transformation begins with us.

It's worth saying that our lives are transformed when we stop relying on ourselves for direction and guidance, when we stop trying to figure out what is right in our own minds, but instead rely on the teachings of Scripture to lead us in a life of faith.

We know that our lives are transformed when we stop relying on ourselves to create a better future, and instead rejoice in the truth that God has been at work in our world, making earth as it is in Heaven, for in God is our hope.

And we believe that God is transforming our lives with the gift of love. He is a God who loves us despite our weakness, a God who calls us to love each other despite our sins and shortcomings.

What this all means is that "Whenever I am weak, then I am strong, because in my weakness I must depend not on myself, but on my God."

And when we think too highly of ourselves, we are fools.

When we think too highly of ourselves, we are like children who don't stop to thank the parents who put food on their plates and keep the lights on in the house.

We sometimes live in the illusion of self-sufficiency, but consider all that we don't know. We can't even cure the common cold.

I've never seen where a hummingbird sleeps. Is it in a nest? Under a leaf?

When we see only the strength of the one who looks back at us in the mirror, we fail to give thanks for the One who put the stars in the night sky. And we fail to rely on the One who is strong when we are weak.

We must remember that "whenever I am weak, then I am strong," for there is danger in relying too heavily on human strength.

The strong keep going in their marriage while it's falling apart, but the weak trust in a Higher Power and ask for help.

The strong face hardship that they can't see their way out of, and break, while the weak call on the ever-present Help in times of trouble. Because they've called on God, they are more than conquerors.

The strong see death as the end, but the weak sing their loud hallelujah even at the grave, giving thanks for the strength of Christ who carries us from death to new life. We give thanks for Christ, who leads us out into an ever-changing world with faith, hope, and love.

That's the symbolism of the acolyte.

The hardest job in a worship service is the job of the acolyte.

It's the only job that involves a flame in an old wooden building. With the acolyte is the greatest potential for something to go badly wrong. But not only that, there are so many variables. The flame could go out on the wand. The wax can melt in the tube and the wick won't light. Every once in a while there won't be enough oil in the candles and they won't light while everyone is watching. Plus, you have to lead the worship leaders into the sanctuary – walking first in line down the aisle in front of your church family. It's a lot of pressure.

Last Sunday some things went wrong.

The light went out on the wand before Emma Grace could make it down to the front. Her dad and I had to run up with the lighter to get things going in the right direction again. But Emma Grace persevered, you see. It was her first time to acolyte in the 11:00 service, and even though everyone was watching, she didn't give up. She persevered, and when I think about life, isn't perseverance more important than strength?

Certainly, it's more attainable than perfection.

Knowing where to go for help matters greatly because no mortal always knows the way.

Having the courage to ask a question is more important in the grand scheme of things because we all hit a point where we don't have the answer.

Perseverance then. Because of her perseverance, at the end of the service, Emma Grace took up the acolyte's wand once again, and with it lit she led us out of this sanctuary, reminding us that the light of Christ goes out into the world with us.

We are not alone, for "whenever I am weak, then I am strong," because Christ gives me strength.

Amen.

About the Author

Rev. Joe Evans was born in Georgia, baptized at Morningside Presbyterian Church in Atlanta, and was confirmed and nurtured by First Presbyterian Church of Marietta, Georgia. He is a graduate of Presbyterian College in Clinton, South Carolina and of Columbia Theological Seminary in Decatur, Georgia. He was ordained into the office of Minister of Word and Sacrament at First Presbyterian Church of Marietta in March of 2007. From ordination to 2010, Rev. Evans served Good Shepherd Presbyterian Church in Lilburn, Georgia as Associate Pastor of Mission and Outreach and as Interim Pastor. From 2011 to 2017, he served First Presbyterian Church in Columbia, Tennessee as Senior Pastor. In July 2017, he was installed as the Senior Pastor of First Presbyterian Church of Marietta, where he continues to live and serve, alongside his wife Sara and their two daughters, Lily and Cece.

Rev. Evans has also served as editor of *Lectionary Homiletics*, contributed to various journals and magazines, and is a frequent preacher on *Day 1*, an internationally syndicated radio program formally known as *the Protestant Hour*.